McWhirter Theory
of
Stock Market Forecasting

Louise McWhirter

No part of this book may be reproduced by any mechanical, photographic, or electronic process, or in the form of a phonographic recording, nor may it be stored in a retrieval system, transmitted, translated into another language or otherwise copied for public or private use, excepting brief passages quoted for purposes of review, without permission of the publisher.

ISBN-10: 0-86690-585-5
ISBN-13: 978-0-86690-585-5

First published in 1938 by Astro Book Company

2008 Edition Published by:
American Federation of Astrologers
6535 S Rural Road
Tempe AZ 85283

www.astrologers.com

Printed in the United States of America

To

The Sincere Students of Astrology

At first, we bask contented in our sun
And take what daylight shows us for the truth.
Then we discover . . .
                        Alfred Noyes

Contents

Introduction	vii
Chapter I, Theory and Application of Forecasting Stock Market Trends	1
Chapter II, Business Cycles and Stock Market Trends, 1850-1950	9
Chapter III, How to Forecast Monthly and Daily Trends on the New York Stock Exchange	95
Chapter IV, How to Forecast Trends of Individual Stocks	111
Chapter V, Date and Place of Incorporation of Stocks Listed on the New York Stock Exchange	133
Glossary	181
Sign Rulership of Countries	193

List of Illustrations

Business Cycle Chart	3
California Gold Prosperity Period, 1850-1854	10
Panic of 1857	12
Secession Depression, 1859-1862	15
War Prosperity Period, 1863-1865	18
Primary Post-War Depression, 1865-1866	20
Industrial Over-Expansion Prosperity Period	24
Secondary Post-War Depression, 1873-1879	28
Gold Resumption Prosperity Period, 1879-1883	31
Depression of 1884	35
Railroad Prosperity Period, 1888-1892	39
Baring Crisis, 1891	42
Panic of 1893-1895	44
Recovery of 1895	47
Silver Campaign Depression, 1896-1897	49
Merger Prosperity Period, 1900-1903	53
Rich Mans Panic, 1903-1904	55
Corporate Prosperity Period, 1905-1907	57
Panic of 1907	60
War Depression, 1913-1914	63
War Prosperity Period. 1915-1918	66
Primary Post-War Depression, 1920-1922	68
Coolidge Prosperity Period, 1925-1927	71
"Bull Market Boom," 1928-1929	74
Secondary Post-War Depression, 1929-1934	76
Chart of the United States of America	90
New York Stock Exchange Chart	96
New York Stock Exchange Chart with Planet Positions for March 2, 1938	103
New York Stock Exchange Chart with Planet Positions for May 29, 1938	106
Example I United States Steel Corporation Chart	113
Example II Spiegel, Inc. Chart	124
Example III Sears Roebuck Company Chart	129

Introduction

By Alphee Lavoie

It's not often these days to find a book that truly offers a solid foundation to a specific field of study; a pioneering book that is so unique, well researched and makes a truly outstanding contribution to a study or topic. Louise McWhirter's book, *McWhirter Theory of Stock Market Forecasting*, is just one of those books. And what makes it even more remarkable is that this little treasure came along more than 70 years ago!

Using astrology to assist in predicting the market is a completely different experience than using astrology in a client consultation.

I strongly believe that every astrologer should spend at least one full year investing their hard-earned money in the stock market using their astrological knowledge before putting up a shingle to signal the public that they are open to see clients for astrological consultations. They would learn very quickly that unless you do your homework, stock market investing with astrology is the fastest way to make a park bench your permanent home!

Many astrologers use astrological concepts that were never researched or validated and, sorry to say, have no real way to discern whether these concepts truly work. Astro-finance quickly and definitively trains you to be sure that the astrological techniques you are using has a high probability of yielding a positive, working re-

Introduction

sult before you employ them. That's why Louise McWhirter's book is vital to our education in the astro financial field. *She has done the research!*

Twenty-five years ago when I began my work in astro finance, Louise McWhirter's book, *McWhirter Theory of Stock Market Forecasting*, was one of the few books that I devoured with intensity. In conducting some of my own research on her theory of nodal cycles and their effects on business cycles, I found it to be incredibly accurate. It is no secret that business cycles run for eighteen years. It just so happens that eighteen years is also the same time that it takes the North Node of the Moon to complete one pass around the zodiac, tying it exactly to the Nodes of the Moon. And today, her lunar Node concept still predicts business cycles with uncanny accuracy.

Another one of her ingenious discoveries was her application of the monthly lunation. She worked with this phenomenon and the New York Stock Exchange chart to make monthly predictions for the reaction of the Dow Jones. When I first read about this method I was startled because it was so foreign to me. It was unlike anything that I had previously learned or used in all my years as a professional astrologer. But she kept to her usual pattern in her own work and thoroughly researched, tested, and produced valid results.

In my forty-five plus years as a professional astrologer I've listened to many lectures on astro finance, and I might add many were way off base. But Louise McWhirter's work proved to me that serious and valid research could produce accurate, viable results.

This was the inspiration and motivation I needed. In 2002, I started a group called The Astro Investigators, fondly called the 'Gators, just for this purpose—to scientifically research through intense investigation what really works and what doesn't. We have a website at www.astroinvestigators.com with many studies, and our mission is to research every technique before employing it in practice.

McWhirter's book is full of useful astro finance information. After reading the book a few times it amazed me as to the amount of hours she must have spent testing these methods. Back in the '20s and '30s when she did her work it was not easy to calculate planetary positions and astrological charts because it was done by hand and required a tremendous amount of time, knowledge, and dedication.

I personally love when authors reveal all, when they don't hide anything or obscure their methods or techniques. I loudly applaud McWhirter for including numerous, clear, step-by-step explanations of the astrological concepts she used to make her stock predictions.

In all my research in astro finance I was curious to find that 14° of cardinality is very strong in the Dow Jones movement. Years ago I rectified the United States chart for July 4, 1776 at 4:58 p.m. EST in Philadelphia. In that chart Saturn is at 14 Libra 48. This chart has the sign Capricorn on the second house of money, so it makes sense that 14° of cardinality would be important in predicting the Dow Jones.

Louise always mentioned that the New York Stock Exchange chart of May 17, 1792 had 14 Cancer rising and a Pisces Midheaven. I immediately knew that the chart she was using was a good one. I spent some time checking the validity of this chart and rectified the time to 7:52 a.m. in New York City.

There are many good authors in this field who have created astro financial methods for the market. But everyone trading the market knows that it is a *must* to check and double-check every technique used for trading.

This book has had a tremendous influence on me. Her intelligent, well-researched work inspired me to move beyond the set limits and boundaries of the field to create the award-winning Market Trader Financial Software programs. And, as a tribute to her, there is much of her methodology and approach to trading utilized in our line of Astro-Financial Software.

Introduction

Louise McWhirter's market trading system ranks among the top few that I know of in the field of financial astrology. Reviving this book and making it available again to the public at large is a true gift. If you are a trader or considering venturing into this exciting field, then this book really needs to be on your bookshelf and I promise you . . . if you read it once, it won't sit on the shelf collecting dust!

Alphee Lavoie
www.alphee.com

Chapter I

Theory and Application of Forecasting Stock Market Trends

The theory of forecasting future trends of the Stock Market and the trend of business, as outlined in this book, is based on sound astronomical law. The law is here; it need only be applied to bring economic independence and a more abundant living to every man and woman in this country.

The way conditions exist today, man is the victim of the business cycle. With detailed charts and graphs, he can tell you when business began to pick up, and when a recession started, but he cannot tell you those factors in advance, with all his statistical research, because he has no *time factor*.

A leading economist, Col. Leonard P. Ayres of the Cleveland Trust Company, in a booklet entitled *Business Recovery Following Depression*, states in a paragraph that "positive forecasting" is impossible despite the fact that all booms and depressions have a certain similarity. There is always a new factor present which was not present in the last depression or previous depressions. To quote:

"The explanation of this lack of uniformity is to be found in the variety of the fundamental conditioning factors that may control the developments and outcomes of these business swings. Chief among these is agricultural production which powerfully affects the general prosperity of the country. War is another controlling factor which cannot be foreseen. The prosperity of peoples in other lands is still another of the influences that powerfully modify conditions in this country.

"Since these and other factors cannot be foretold, it is impossible to construct a reliable method for making statistical forecasts of finance and business."

The theory of this book, however, makes the forecasting with accuracy of all of the above hitherto unknown factors, by the study of the angular relation of the planetary bodies to each other as they transit the twelve signs of the zodiac.

It is a fact that certain countries are "ruled" by certain signs of the zodiac. That is, from observation and research, it has been found that a planet passing through a certain sign has a very definite bearing on the fortunes of a particular country. For example, the United States is strongly under the influence of the signs Gemini and Cancer, and planets passing through these two signs have a very definite effect upon the business conditions of this country, depending of course on the nature of the planet. These planetary transits can be known years in advance. The same is true of war conditions, crop conditions, booms, recessions, etc., the angular relation of the planetary bodies forecasting the conditions.

The ecliptic is the Sun's path. A planet crossing this path moves from South latitude to North latitude and from North latitude to South latitude. The word "node" is the name for the points in the orbit of a planet where it crosses the Ecliptic, or Sun's path. The point where it crosses from south to north is the North Node; and the point where it crosses from north to south is called the South Node. The Moon's Nodes have a cycle of nineteen years. That is, it takes them nineteen years to pass through the twelve signs of the

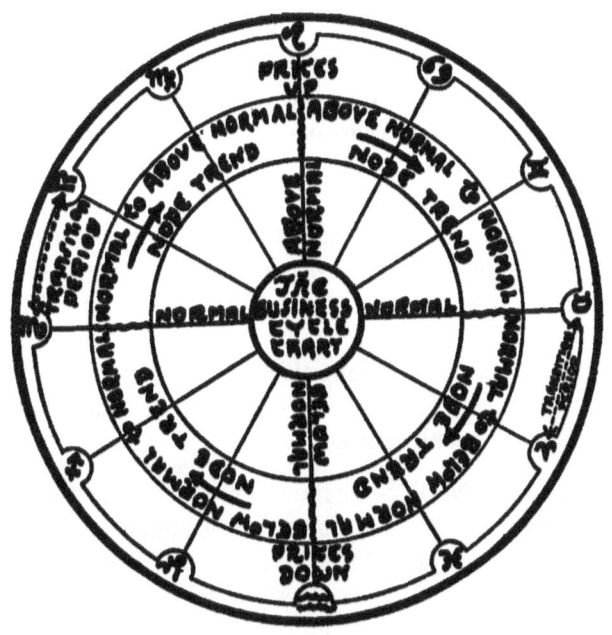

Business Cycle Chart

zodiac. The trend of the Business Volume Curve has been found to correspond with the cycle of the North Node. In this theory, the transit of the North Node forms the basic trend of business activity and volume. Secondary planetary factors can distort this Curve ten to twenty per cent above or below the normal line, depending upon the nature of the planet and the angles formed. Business Cycles, as portrayed on the Chart *"A Century of Business Progress"* by Col. Leonard P. Ayres, is used on a comparative basis with the transit of the North Node portraying the major trend of business volume and activity. Planetary aspects or angles to the North Node and to each other form the secondary trend. In other words, the major trend of Business Activity is clearly shown by the movement of the North Node around the Business Cycle Chart.

Whenever the North Node passes through Scorpio and Libra (the North Node moves backward through the zodiac), business goes through an approximate three year "transition period," if there are no unfavorable secondary factors present to distort the Business Activity Curve; business volume is going from normal to above normal, creating a prosperity period or the beginning of a Bull Market in stock prices as well as other forms of business. Whenever the North Node reaches the sign of Leo, Business Volume is normally at a high point, if there are no secondary factors present of an unfavorable nature to distort the Curve. As the North Node passes through Cancer and Gemini, Business Volume is above normal, but the trend is slowly toward normal. Favorable secondary factors can prolong this prosperity period beyond the allotted time and unfavorable secondary factors can decrease the length of the favorable period.

Whenever the North Node moves into Taurus, a "transition period" begins which lasts through the sign of Aries, which is approximately three years. This is a warning that the normal position of the Business Volume Curve has been reached and that the trend of Business activity is slowly going from normal to below normal for the next three or four years.

In 1929, the North Node was in Taurus and had been there since December 1928, giving the warning six to eight months in advance that the Bull Market Boom was nearing its end. Jupiter was in Taurus in conjunction with the North Node in May and June of 1929, a favorable secondary factor which sent the Business Curve upward six points through June. However, when this aspect passed, the Curve dropped and remained below normal for four years until the North Node passed out of the sign Aquarius, which is the sign on the low point of the Business Cycle Chart. According to this theory all these factors were predictable in advance years ahead of the actual happening. No Administration was responsible for the Depression and no Administration is responsible for the Recovery according to this theory, which is based on the Law of Action and Reaction. The "real" recovery began in February 1935, when the North Node moved out of Aquarius, the sign on the low point of the Business Cycle Chart. A favorable secondary factor,

Saturn sextile Uranus, was also present during a two-year period and this sent stock market prices and business activity higher than they normally would have been. In August 1937, when the present recession set in, the North Node was in Sagittarius, and the normal position of the Business Volume Curve was slightly below normal. At the same time Saturn placed on the Midheaven of the New York Stock Exchange Chart indicated lower prices for stocks and bonds. When this planet formed an unfavorable forty-five degree angle to Uranus, Stock Market prices began to plummet.

In April 1938, Saturn moved to a slightly favorable angle with Uranus (thirty degrees) and the North Node moved into Scorpio, the transition point on the Business Cycle Chart, indicating that the technical "normal" point has been reached by the Business Curve, and with the slightly favorable secondary factor present, stocks should go up next year as Jupiter passes over the Midheaven of the New York Stock Exchange Chart, and Business Volume should rise toward the normal line during most of 1939.

The Theory

The major or primary trend of business volume and finance is clearly pointed out by the nineteen-year cycle of the North Node as it passes through the twelve signs of the zodiac.

Whenever the North Node passes through Scorpio and Libra, there is a transition period as the Curve passes from normal, going from normal to high.

The high point of business volume is reached when the North Node transits Leo. As the North Node goes through Cancer and Gemini, Business volume is above normal, but slowly going to normal.

Taurus is the transition point or normal point as the Curve goes from normal to below normal in business volume.

When the North Node enters Aquarius, the low point of Business activity has been reached. As the Node transits Capricorn and

Sagittarius, the normal position of the Business Curve is below normal going to normal.

This is the natural position of the Curve without the presence of secondary factors which can distort the Curve favorably or unfavorably from one to twenty percent.

The following secondary factors have been found to lift the Business Curve:

1. Jupiter conjunction the North Node.
2. Saturn trine, sextile, or semi-sextile Uranus.
3. Jupiter in Gemini or Cancer.
4. Jupiter in conjunction, sextile or trine aspect to Saturn and Uranus, which are in aspect to each other.
5. The North Node in Gemini.
6. Favorable aspects to Pluto.

The following secondary factors have been found to depress the Business Curve:

1. Saturn conjunction the North Node; square or opposition to it.
2. Saturn conjunction, square, opposition, or semi-square Uranus.
3. Saturn in Gemini.
4. Uranus in Gemini.
5. Uranus square, conjunction, opposition the North Node.
6. Unfavorable aspects to Pluto.

A combination of any of these factors give strength for whatever they indicate. If one or more favorable secondary factors are present they take the Curve upward. If one or more unfavorable secondary factors are present they turn the Curve downward. If one good and one unfavorable secondary factor are also present, the effect of the secondary factors is to neutralize each other, or to counteract the effects of the various factors involved.

The New York Stock Exchange

The trend of stock market prices tends to conform to the major trend of the Business Curve. However, the Stock Market is under a set of individual conditions of its own. These governing planetary factors may be told by studying the Chart of the New York Stock Exchange as originated by the writer. Planets on the angles of the New York Stock Exchange Chart clearly indicate Market conditions. Aspects favorable and unfavorable between Saturn and Uranus or Pluto, definitely indicate stock trends; and aspects between Mars and Neptune, the two planetary rulers of the Midheaven of the New York Stock Exchange Chart, and the aspects from other major planets to Mars and Neptune, indicate what the Stock Market price averages will do. These are taken up in detail in Chapter III. Chapter II shows how Stock Market trends and Business Cycles are correlated.

Application

The practical application of this theory should bring economic independence to a greater number of people than ever before. It shows how to analyze, years in advance, business conditions; crops, wars, and other factors which have such an important effect upon security prices. It shows you when to get out of the Market and when to get in, which are two of the more important things a trader must know.

Everything needed for the study of this theory is contained in this book and can be practically applied.

The rise and fall of Stock Market prices come in definite intervals of time or cycles which follow the Curve of Business Volume and activity. This rise and fall of prices is governed by the law of supply and demand, which in turn is governed by a law in the universe, hitherto unknown or ignored, known as the Law of Action and Reaction. Periods of business prosperity and depression are not man-made nor the result of chance; they come at regular intervals, the same as the seasons, and the same astronomical laws which govern nature, govern man and all of man's activities. When this fact is recognized, man will work in harmony with the forces of nature and not blindly against them.

At the present time, a planned investment program based on the laws of nature which govern supply and demand is an unheard of thing. It is not, however, an impossibility in the near future. When man turns from disturbing political factors long enough to see that business volume and the fluctuations of the Stock Market defy Administrative control, they will begin to wonder what is the law behind it all. No Administration can make depression and no Administration can make prosperity. Business Cycles occur of their own accord at regular intervals despite the Government. However, by acknowledging the law of nature behind this theory, administrative heads in the future can plan ahead for depressions and not be caught in the midst of prosperity by a changed Business Cycle and a financial panic. When this sort of preparedness takes place, the time will come when there are no depressions because man has already prepared for a rainy day and has more than enough to tide him over lean years. When the Cycle changes and the Business Curve starts upward again, man will be able to invest again and like the farmer watch his seed grow. It is no longer necessary to be wiped out on the Stock Market. *That* is a sign of ignorance.

Chapter II

Business Cycles and Stock Market Trends 1850-1950

The California Gold Inflation Prosperity Period

This period takes in the years of 1850 to 1854 inclusively. Reference to a table called an Ephemeris, which gives the geocentric planetary positions for this period, shows that the North Node is in Leo, the sign which is on the highest point of the Business Cycle Chart. Since the Node indicates the trend or curve of business activity and volume as it passes through the respective twelve signs on the chart, it is easy to see that for business activity and volume this period was characterized by "above normal prices."

In 1850, prices rose from Normal to 11 points above Normal in January 1851. During 1851 prices began to drop due to the influence as shown by the conjunction of the planet Saturn and Uranus, secondary factors, which can distort the Business Activity Curve from 10 percent to 20 percent either way depending upon the nature of the aspect. This aspect was very unfavorable and prices dropped in stocks and bonds as well as business until October 1851, when these planets had moved out of orb of each other. Since the Node was still in Leo, indicating that business volume would increase as soon as the secondary factor was out of the way,

Business Cycles and Stock Market Trends 1850-1950

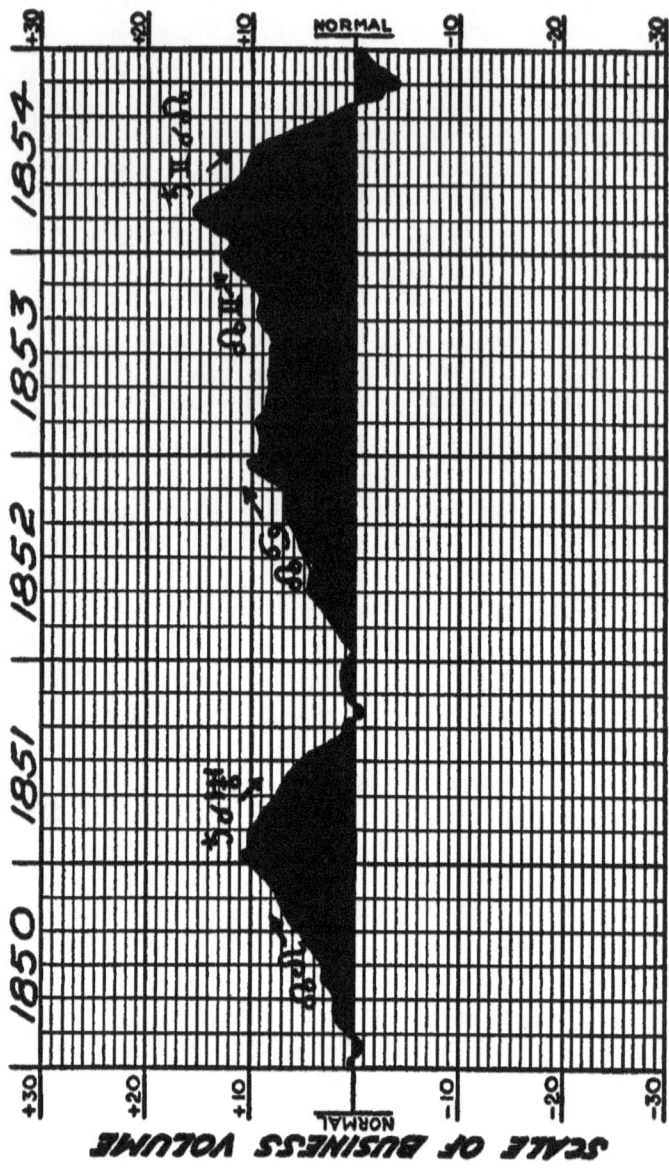

California Gold Prosperity Period, 1850-1854

prices began to go up, and prices had a steady climb through 1852, reaching 10 points above normal in business activity. The year 1853 saw business volume eight points above normal and the curve going to a high of 15 points above normal through March 1854.

In April of 1854, another secondary factor appeared to cause a temporary business recession. Saturn moved into the sign of Gemini which rules the United States. This in itself would cause business volume to recede, but it also happens that the Node moving backward in its orbit had also gone into the sign of Gemini. Saturn in conjunction with the North Node caused the Business Curve to turn downward sharply, reaching a low of four points below Normal in December 1854. Stock prices also dropped during this period.

As the North Node goes from Leo to Taurus on the Business Cycle Chart, it is easy to see that the Curve of Business activity is going slowly but surely from "Above Normal" to "Normal." In other words, in the midst of so-called prosperity the influence is slowly at work which will swing the trend of business in the opposite direction, after the Node reaches the sign of Taurus, which is the transition point, as prices and the Business Curve work slowly from "Normal" to "Below Normal" in prices.

The Panic of 1857

In June of 1854 the North Node passed in Taurus, which indicated that the Economic Curve of business was now moving slowly from "Normal" to "Below Normal." The period of passing through the signs of Taurus and Aries was a Transition Period and marks the years from 1854 to 1857 as a Transition Era, despite the fact that business volume was 10 points above Normal during the middle of 1856. This was due to the presence of a favorable secondary factor, Jupiter in Pisces. Pisces is the sign which governs the topmost point on the chart of the New York Stock Exchange and shows business conditions at large. Jupiter was also in con-

Business Cycles and Stock Market Trends 1850-1950

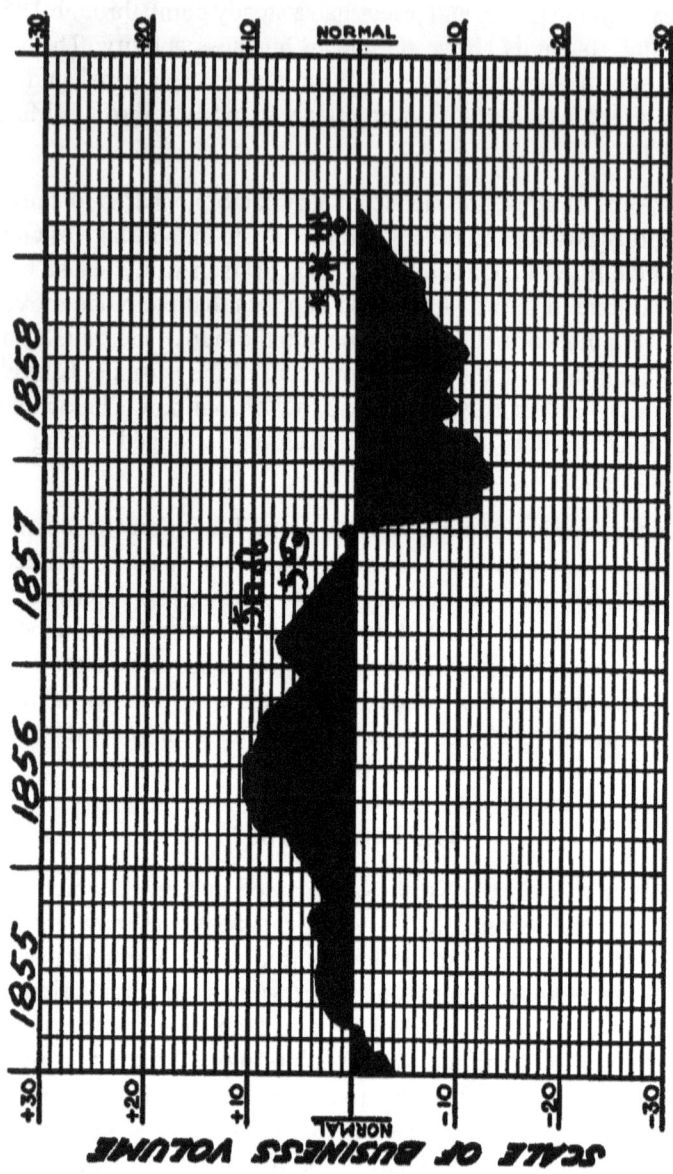

Panic of 1857

junction with the North Node and with Neptune, the planetary ruler of Pisces. The combination of these factors showed the above normal business activity during 1856. Stocks were up and business was very good.

In February 1857, Saturn was square the North Node, although Jupiter was in conjunction with it. This caused a drop of three points in Business volume and as Saturn was in Cancer during all of 1857 it was passing over the Ascendant of the chart of the New York Stock Exchange, a critical point for showing action on the New York Stock Exchange. Stock prices dropped all spring and summer and business volume shrank during this period, culminating in the fall in a sharp drop which carried business volume thirteen points below Normal. This was known as the Panic of 1837. Economists attribute this Panic to over-development in the West and excessive railroad construction during this period. The Panic was dearly shown, however, by the fact that the lunation *(conjunction of the Sun and Moon every twenty-eight days)* for September fell in 25 degrees Virgo in exact opposition to the Midheaven of the New York Stock Exchange and in exact opposition to the North Node, and Neptune also, in the Midheaven of this Chart in 27 and 21 degrees of Pisces respectively.

Referring to the Business Cycle Chart, it is easy to see that Pisces is the sign next to the lowest for business activity and prices, and that the Business Curve was now "Below Normal."

The effect of the Panic of 1857 was felt throughout 1858, with business volume from ten to six points below normal.

In February 1859, the North Node moved into the sign of Aquarius, which is the sign on the lowest point of the Business Cycle Chart. This indicates that the Business Curve was at its lowest point with prices below normal. However, a glance at the graph depicting business volume for the period shows that business hovered from two points above normal to two points below normal in activity; therefore, some strong secondary factor must have been present which indicated that prices and business volume were up to normal. This was the condition present during 1859, and it was depicted by Saturn in Leo sextile Uranus in Gemini. It was during this time that the Atlantic submarine cable was laid.

This aspect came into force in August 1858 and pointed to a rise in business volume from the lows of the Panic of 1857. This aspect was effective throughout 1859, and indicated that business activity would reach normal.

Neptune, which is one of the planetary rulers, or significators, of the New York Stock Exchange, was in 28 degrees Pisces, the Midheaven of the New York Stock Exchange Chart, during 1860 and trine Jupiter in Cancer on the Ascendant of the Chart. The Ascendant and Midheaven are two of the most important angles of the Chart in relation to stock market trends and general business activity. Since this aspect was favorable, it pointed to a rise in business generally. The business curve rose five points above normal through July 1860. This was the high point of this secondary trend as Saturn moved into Virgo on August 26, 1860, and in this position was approaching a square aspect with Uranus. This was a signal that the trend had changed and that the averages of stocks were going down and business activity with it.

The Secession Depression

Prices dropped steadily through the fall of 1860 and through the spring and summer of 1861, as indicated by the culmination of a square aspect between Saturn in Virgo and Uranus in Gemini.

On the Business Cycle Chart, the Node had moved into Capricorn August 31, 1860, and remained in this sign through 1861, passing into Sagittarius March 19, 1862. The cycle of the North Node from Aquarius, the Low point, to Scorpio, the Normal point, indicated that business activity was below Normal going to Normal, during this period and with the passing of the secondary factors of an unfavorable nature, business would rapidly go back to Normal.

McWhirter Theory of Stock Market Forecasting

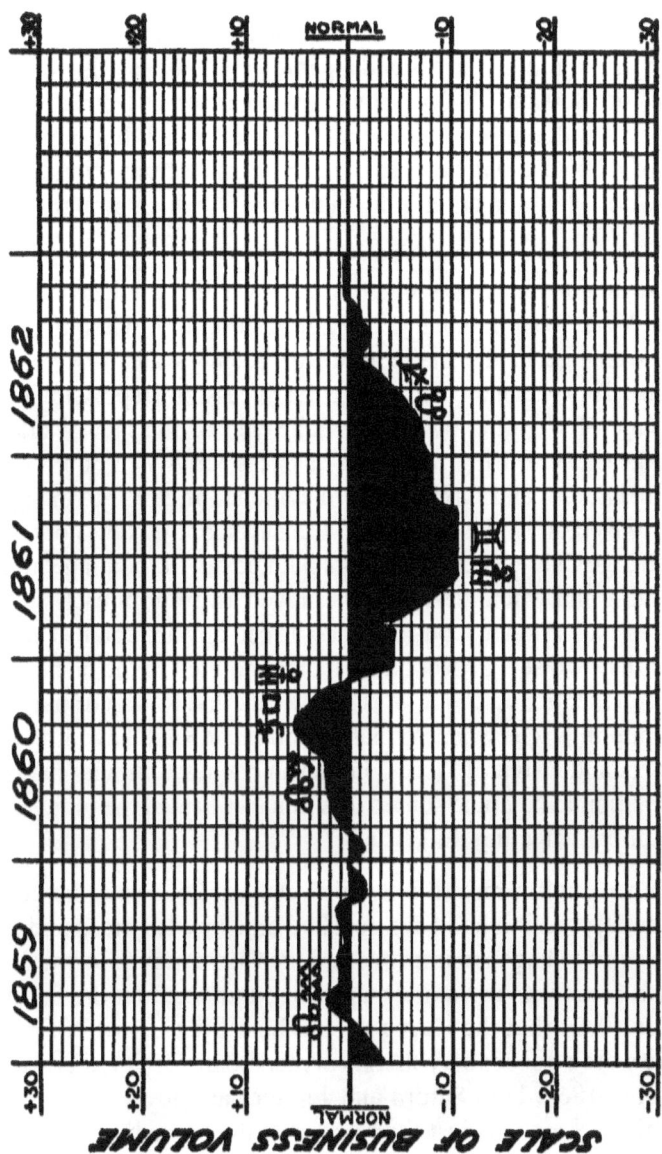

The Secession Depression, 1859-1962

Business Cycles and Stock Market Trends 1850-1950

South Carolina seceded from the Union on December 20, 1860, and the crash came which was followed by a slump in business, a drop in commodity prices and a panic in rail issues. This financial crisis of 1860 and 1861 was the most severe crisis from a business failure standpoint that this country had ever had, but the depression did not last long because of the business activity stimulated by the Civil War, and other industrial activity, which brought higher prices.

No major planet has ever passed over the Midheaven of the New York Stock Exchange or in opposition to it without indicating a change in the major trend of business and stock market prices. This was indicated during the Secession Depression by the passage of Neptune over the Midheaven of the New York Exchange Chart. During 1861 with business activity 11 points below normal Saturn and Jupiter were in conjunction in Virgo in opposition to Neptune in Pisces on the Midheaven of the New York Stock Exchange Chart. These indicators pointed out the coming slump in business and when these aspects moved away from each other, it was an indication that business had turned upward again. Thus it is seen that two sets of secondary factors pointed to the business recession mentioned above. It is significant that Railroad shares had a slump in prices when so many prominent Rails have important planets in the sign of Pisces. Jupiter in conjunction with Saturn in opposition to Neptune square to Uranus indicated the unfavorable conditions affecting Rail issues.

When Jupiter moved into Libra August 25, 1862, the bottom of the Depression had been reached and slowly prices and business activity began to improve and the Curve moved upward. The North Node was in Sagittarius, which indicated on the Business Cycle Chart that the Curve should be a little below Normal, if there were no secondary factors present to distort it either way. In October 1862, both Saturn and Jupiter had moved into Libra, a position which was just the reverse of the preceding indications of lower prices, and it was easy to see from these favorable indicators that business activity should revert to Normal during 1863, especially since the North Node had moved very near to the sign of Scorpio, which represents Normal levels on the Business Cycle Chart.

Jupiter in Libra was trine Uranus in Gemini most of 1863 and this good secondary factor increased prices and the Business Curve went four points above Normal. In the late fall Mars moved into Libra, and since Libra is a transition sign for all planets on the Business Cycle Chart, and Mars is generally an adverse planet when using this method of studying the Business Curve, a slight dip in business activity took place during December.

War Prosperity

On October 7, 1863, the North Node moved into the sign of Scorpio, which is the sign on the Business Cycle Chart that indicates business activity had reached the Normal level. At the same time Saturn was rapidly approaching a trine aspect with Uranus. This was a strong secondary factor present which would distort the Curve approximately 10 percent. On the graph depicting business volume for the period, business activity rose 10 percent above Normal! This aspect lasted through April 1864, when the New Moon of April 6, 1864, fell in 16 degrees Aries on the Midheaven of the New York Stock Exchange Chart in opposition to Saturn in 14 degrees Libra. This indication pointed to a sharp drop in business activity and stock market prices during April, which according to the graph, showed a drop of seven points in business activity.

If the good secondary factor of Saturn trine Uranus had not still been in force, business activity would have had a more severe recession at this time than it did have. This aspect kept in force indicated that prices would still be slightly above Normal. They remained from 3 to 4 points above Normal during the remainder of 1864. Commodity prices were up at this time along with stock and bond prices.

Business Cycles and Stock Market Trends 1850-1950

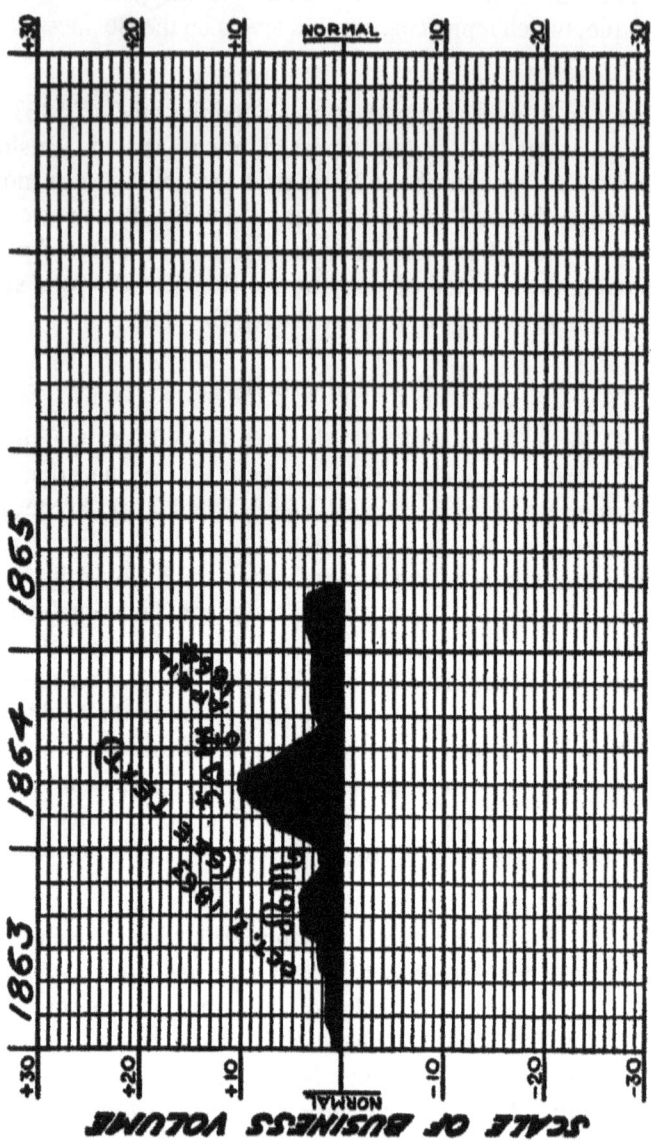

War Prosperity Period, 1863-1865

Primary Post-War Depression

On January 21, 1865, the depressing planet Saturn moved into the sign of Scorpio. This was an indication that business activity was in for a slump, since the North Node was also in Scorpio, the sign on the Normal angle of the Business Cycle Chart. As this aspect became exact, lasting through October of the same year, the crash came and business volume tumbled 14 points below Normal under this strong secondary aspect. Jupiter was also in opposition to Uranus during this period adding weight to the above testimony. These indications pointed clearly to the sharp reaction during the year.

As the North Node moved into the sign of Libra on April 28, 1863, Saturn had also moved back into the sign of Libra, holding the aspect in force until late fall. The North Node's transit into Libra indicated that the Business volume Curve was now going from Normal to Above Normal, and that if no unfavorable secondary factors were present to keep the Curve downward, business activity should be slightly Above Normal for this period.

On September 30, 1865, Saturn moved into Scorpio again, this time forming a trine aspect with Uranus in Cancer. Prices and business turned sharply upward with business volume rising 14 points to Normal by the end of February 1866. This rise in the Business Curve continued through September 1866, with the favorable aspect indicating that business volume would go 10 percent above normal, which it did.

As it has been stated before in this astronomic theory of forecasting business and stock market trends, as long as a major planet is passing over the Midheaven of the New York Exchange Chart, this planet is the "key" for studying business indications for the future for as long as the planet transits the Midheaven. Monthly trends in the Stock Market can be easily determined by watching the lunations each twenty-eight days. If the lunation falls conjunction, square, or in opposition to the planet passing over the Midheaven, watch out, for the Stock Market will then react ac-

Business Cycles and Stock Market Trends 1850-1950

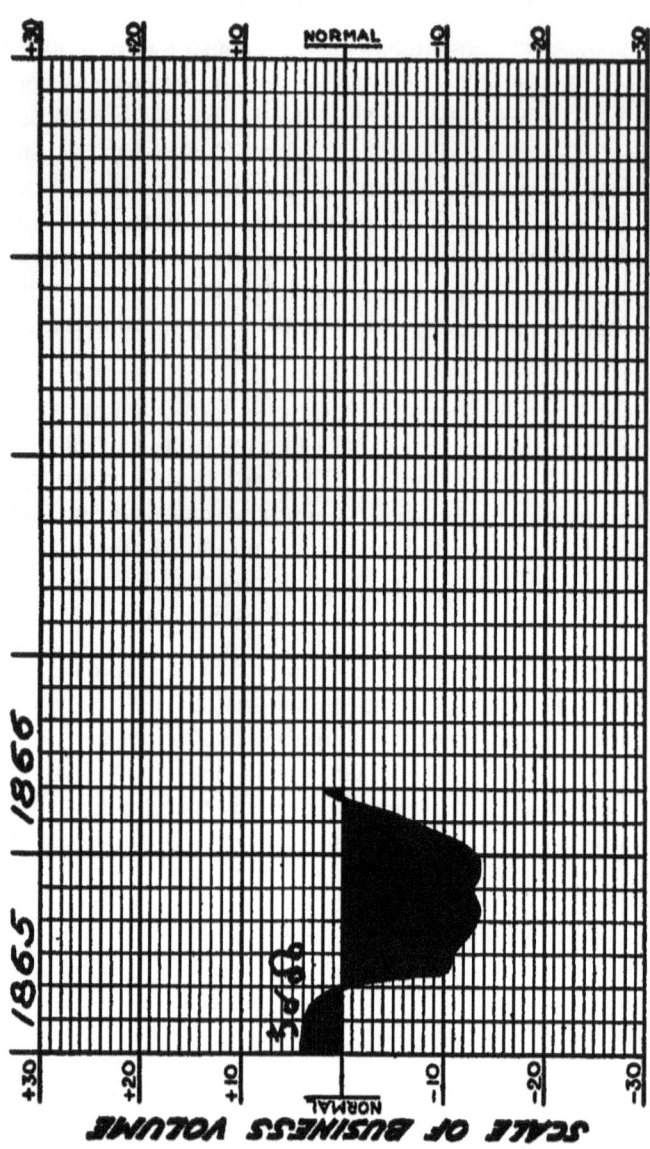

Primary Post-War Depression, 1865-1866

cording to the indications at the lunation, when the Moon passes over that important point, during the forthcoming month.

This theory of forecasting business trends and stock market action explains clearly why so many Stock Market crashes and slumps have come in April and October rather than in other months of the year. The Sun transits the sign of Aries every year from March 21 to April 20, and this is the sign which is co-ruler with Pisces of the Midheaven of the Chart of the New York Stock Exchange. The Sun transits the sign of Libra every year from September 23 to October 23, and this is the sign which is in exact opposition to Aries. Whenever there is a major planet passing through Aries and the lunation falls conjunction *(as in April)* or in opposition to it *(as in September and October)*, then the Market slumps come.

England is ruled by the sign Aries, and it is significant that the transits of major planets through this sign or in opposition to it affect its business conditions and point out the rise and fall of its stock prices very clearly. The tie-up between the London Exchange and Wall Street is shown by the rulership of Aries on the Midheaven of the New York Stock Exchange Chart. Slumps in London have a sympathetic recession here and vice versa.

To return to 1866, history records a financial panic in London in the spring of that year. Neptune was in 11 degrees Aries in October 1866. The lunation for October 1866, fell in 14 degrees Libra in opposition to Neptune on the Midheaven of the New York Stock Exchange Chart in square aspect to Uranus in Cancer and in exact square to the Ascendant of the same chart in 14 degrees Cancer. This lunation indicated a slump in business and stock prices which took the Curve downward ten points by the end of the year. The latter part of December 1866, saw a minor unfavorable aspect between Saturn in 20 degrees Scorpio and Uranus in 7 degrees Cancer. This was the sesquiquadrate aspect of 135 degrees. Although not very important usually, it was strong enough to help keep business activity four points below normal, accentuating the unfavorable aspect, Neptune square Uranus and the Ascendant, of the Stock Market Chart. This influence lasted through February 1867, and was accompanied by a drop in commodity prices and a decided recession in rail stock prices.

On November 13, 1866, the North Node moved into the sign of Virgo and the natural position of the Business Curve should be slightly above Normal and the trend of business from "Normal to High." *(The High point being reached as the North Node transits Leo in 1868 and 1869.)*

The North Node remained in Virgo throughout 1867. The secondary factor, Saturn sesquiquadrate Uranus, was effective through February 1867. Then prices rose along with improved business activity through the spring and summer to three points above Normal due to the slight aspect, though not close enough to bring a big rise in business activity, of Saturn trine Uranus. After August of this year, the Curve turned downward to four points below Normal through February 1868, as the sesquiquadrate aspect came into force again. After February 1868, Business volume increased and by August 1868, the Business Curve had risen four points above Normal or a rise of six points on the graph in five months time. This was due to the fact that Saturn had moved into Sagittarius and too far away from Uranus for an aspect to be effective. This indicated that a change in trend was coming and that it would be upward with the removal of the secondary factors distorting the Curve at that time. The Business Curve confirms this indication. It stayed three to four points above Normal through the remainder of the year. This influence carried the Curve upward through June 1869, to five points above Normal. By this time Uranus had reached 17 degrees Cancer, the Ascendant of the New York Stock Exchange chart and was in square to Neptune in 19 degrees Aries on the Midheaven of this same chart. Prices slowly turned down with the Business Curve through the summer as Jupiter was in exact square to the North Node.

On September 6, 1869, the lunation occurred in 13 degrees

Virgo in quincunx aspect to Neptune on the Midheaven (of the New York Exchange Chart) and this unfavorable aspect of exactly 150 degrees indicated the short-lived Panic of 1869, which occurred on September 24, 1869. This Panic was mostly a Wall Street affair. Stocks had advanced to high levels from the long period of speculation since the War and a reaction set in. Money rates were at their highest level since 1857 and 1860. Since this Panic occurred on Friday, this slump has gone down in financial history as the "Black Friday Panic."

With the passing of the temporary unfavorable aspect, the Curve began to rise and by June 1870 had climbed to four points above Normal. In May 1870, Jupiter moved into Gemini, which is the sign ruling the United States. This is a very favorable secondary factor and prices should have jumped sharply up and carried the Business Curve with it, if there had not been an unfavorable secondary factor present.

The North Node had moved into Cancer on December 22, 1869, and by June had reached a conjunction aspect with the revolutionary and disturbing planet Uranus. This aspect caused the Business Curve to drop five points below normal. By October 1870, the influence of this unfavorable secondary factor had waned. Uranus was in 26 degrees Cancer and the North Node was in 14 degrees Cancer. *(Conjunction aspects are not elective outside of an orb of 10 degrees).* This fact should be kept in mind for in this theory of determining the Business and Stock Market trend, aspects coming into a ten degree range point to changes in trend many months in advance.

Industrial Over-Expansion Prosperity Period

The Business Curve turned sharply upward after October 1870 and by April 1871 was standing at six points above normal. This was the beginning of the three-year period known in financial history as the "Industrial Over-Expansion Prosperity Period." Jupiter was in Gemini, the sign ruling the United States, in favorable as-

Business Cycles and Stock Market Trends 1850-1950

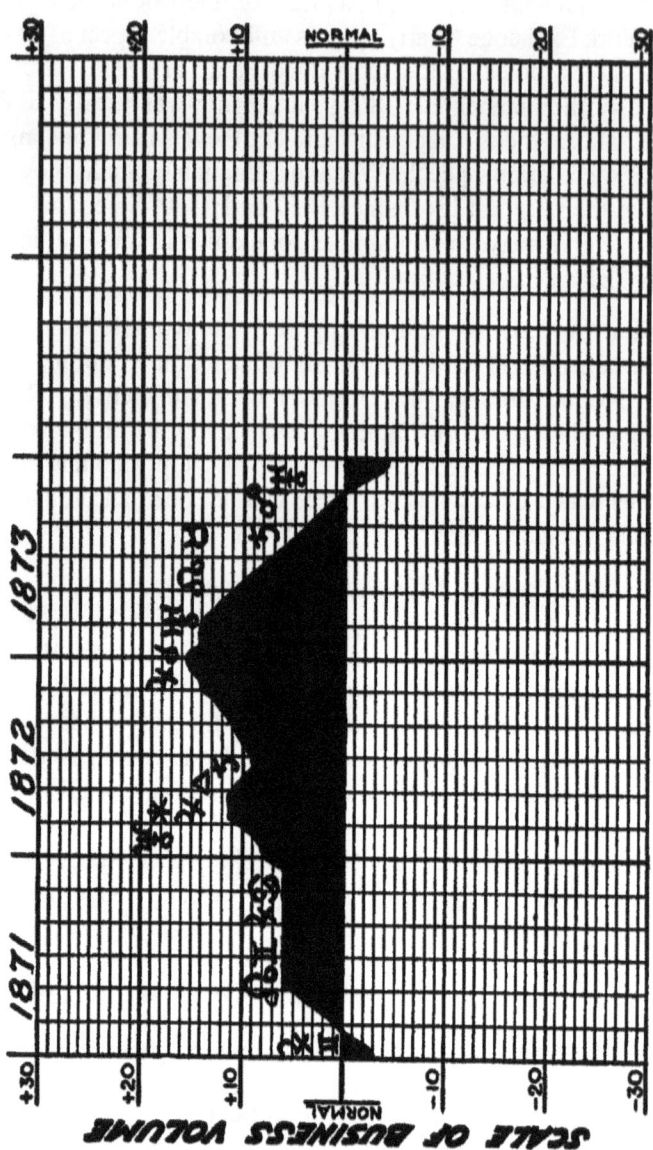

Industrial Over-Expansion Prosperity Period

pect *(sextile* 60 *degrees)* to Neptune in Aries on the Midheaven of the New York Stock Exchange chart and to Uranus in Cancer on the Ascendant of this same chart.

During this period business activity was greatly above normal. Railroads were expanding and being built everywhere. Most Rail stocks come under the influence of the fire signs, Aries, Leo, and Sagittarius. Neptune was in Aries at this time in very favorable aspect *(trine,* 120 *degrees)* to Saturn in Sagittarius and to Jupiter in Gemini (60 *degrees, sextile).* Rail stocks experienced peak prices under these influences.

In May 1871, Jupiter moved into Cancer and in July of the same year, the North Node moved into Gemini. These were favorable indications of a booming business period. Both Gemini and Cancer are the ruling signs of the United States. Whenever beneficent planets or the North Node transits these signs there is always improved business activity, unless some very strong unfavorable secondary factor is present to hold the Curve downward.

The Business Volume Curve stood at six points above normal from April through November 1871. In December the Curve turned upward again, rising sharply through January, February, and March 1872. This upturn was pointed out by the fact that Jupiter was in conjunction with Uranus in Cancer, a strong secondary factor which indicated bullish prices, and lifted the Business Curve to 11 points above normal.

In April 1872, Neptune was still on the Midheaven of the New York Stock Exchange Chart in 23 degrees Aries; Uranus 27 degrees Cancer was in conjunction with Jupiter in 22 degrees Cancer and Saturn was in 21 degrees Capricorn. This was an unusual planetary arrangement with four major planets all placed on angles of the New York Stock Exchange Chart and in square aspect and in opposition to each other. If the primary Curve of Business had not been above normal during this period, augmented by a strong secondary factor of Jupiter conjunction Uranus in Cancer, this combination of aspects would have pointed to a slump in business. As it was, however, the North Node was in Gemini, a very favorable factor, which pointed to an above normal position for the Business Curve, and in consequence only a slight recession took place while these aspects lasted.

The lunation of April 8, 1872 occurred in 18 degrees Aries conjunction Mars and Neptune in Aries, the two planetary rulers of the Midheaven of the New York Stock Exchange Chart. This lunation indicated the slight recession which caused the Business Curve to drop three points. This recession lasted until the last of June when Uranus and Jupiter both moved into Leo.

This placed both planets in favorable aspect (60 *degrees, sextile)* to the North Node in Gemini. This caused the Business Curve to turn upward with boom proportions. Jupiter in conjunction with Uranus doubled the influence of the favorable secondary factor, Jupiter sextile the Node, and the Curve turned sharply upward through the remainder of 1872. The Business Curve reached the top of this boom in January 1873, when it stood at 15 points above normal.

On January 28, 1873, the North Node moved into Taurus, one of the transition points on the Business Cycle Chart and this was a definite indication that the trend had turned downward for a period of six years or the time it took for the North Node to pass through the signs Taurus, Aries, Pisces, and Aquarius, the last being the sign on the low point of the Business Cycle Chart.

From June 4, 1868 to January 28, 1873, the North Node had passed through Leo *(the top point of the Business Cycle Chart),* Cancer, and Gemini. The Business Curve was above normal during this period with the trend slowly approaching normal. When the Normal point was reached, as the North Node moved into Taurus, the cycle had definitely changed. The Curve had now swung downward. This was the beginning of a period in financial history known as the "Secondary Post-War Depression" which lasted for a period of six years.

The Secondary Post-War Depression Period

On March 14, 1873, Saturn moved into the sign of Aquarius, forming a very unfavorable aspect *(opposition, 180 degrees)* with Uranus in 2 degrees Leo. This secondary factor indicated that this country was due for a financial depression of large proportions; a fact which was indicated six months in advance of the actual crash on September 18, 1873, following the failures of the then well-known firms of Kenyon, Cox and Co., the New York Warehouse and Security Co. and Jay Cook and Co. This was one of the worst panics since the War Between the States as it was both a commercial and a Stock Exchange panic. On September 20, 1873, the New York Stock Exchange closed its doors for the first time in history and remained closed for ten days.

Was the crash of September 18, 1873 predictable in advance? Yes, by this theory of forecasting the Stock Market, it was.

Monthly trend changes are pointed out at the lunation which occurs each month at an interval of twenty-eight days. The lunation is the conjunction of the Sun and Moon or the "New Moon" each month. September 18, 1873 occurred three days before the lunation for September; therefore, the crash of September 18, 1873 was shown in the preceding lunation for August, which fell on August 22, 1873 in 29 degrees Leo in square aspect (90 *degrees)* to Mars *(one of the planetary rulers of the Midheaven of the New York Stock Exchange Chart)* and in square aspect to Pluto and the North Node, which were also in conjunction with each other. Any planet in conjunction with the North Node has a marked effect on business activity and Stock Market trends and if it is present it is a secondary factor that must always be taken into account when analyzing business conditions or the Stock Market averages.

The presence of this secondary factor, Pluto in conjunction with the North Node, indicated a decided change coming in the trend of business and Stock Market prices. Taurus is one of the signs of transition on the Business Cycle Chart and since it is the sign showing the trend from "Normal" to "Below Normal" business,

Business Cycles and Stock Market Trends 1850-1950

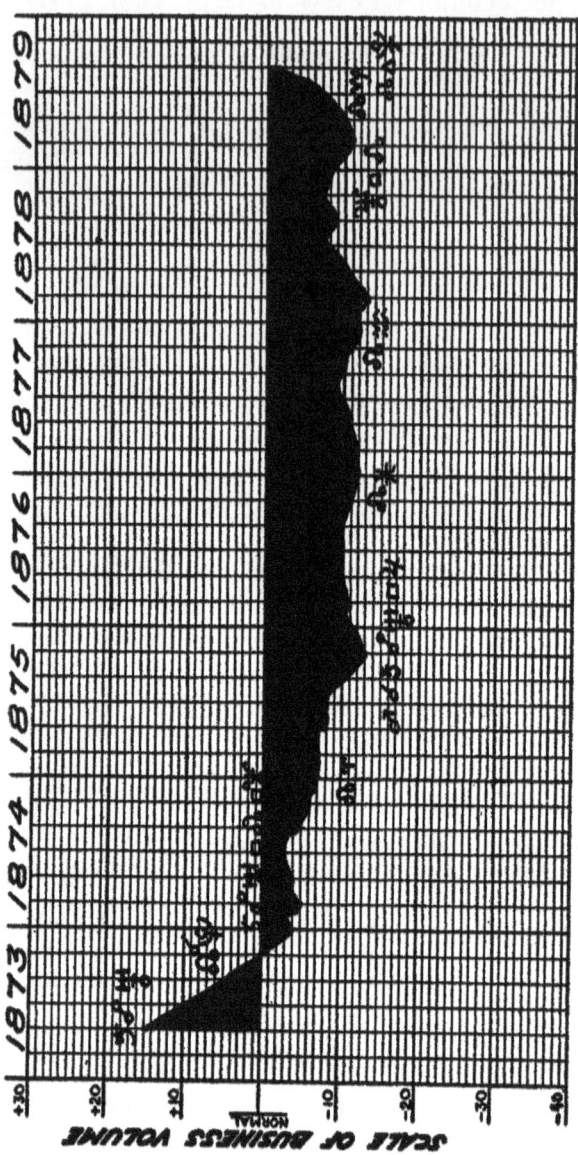

Secondary Post-War Depression, 1873-1879

this aspect corroborated other testimony that the country was on the verge of a financial crisis accompanied by a slump on the New York Stock Exchange. The crash, however, did not come until the Moon passed over 29 degrees Leo, which occurred on September 18, 1873. The Business Curve dropped during the year from a high in March of 15 points above normal to five points below normal.

The Business Curve continued to move downward all during 1874 and 1875, until at the end of 1875 business activity was standing at 15 points below normal. During the first half of 1874, Uranus and Saturn were in opposition to each other and in square aspect (90 *degrees)* to the North Node and Neptune, one of the rulers of the New York Stock Exchange Chart.

On August 16, 1874, the North Node moved into the sign of Aries and the economic curve was downward in trend until the "Below Normal" point was reached on September 22, 1877, when the North Node moved into Aquarius, which is the sign on the low point of the Business Cycle Chart.

Rail stocks were at a low ebb during 1874. Cotton and wheat prices also were depressed and a record number of failures took place. During October, November, and December 1874, the North Node was in conjunction with Neptune, an unfavorable secondary factor which was manifested in a two point drop of the Business Curve which was carried through 1875.

In the fall of 1875, the Business Activity Curve turned downward six points as Mars and Jupiter formed unfavorable aspects to the unfavorable secondary factor *(Saturn in Aquarius in opposition to Uranus in Leo),* already in existence. Mars was in conjunction with Saturn opposition Uranus, and Jupiter was in square aspect to all three planets.

The depression carried through 1876 and 1877, as the North Node entered Aquarius, the low point on the Business Cycle Chart. The North Node in Aquarius was in opposition to Uranus in Leo and this secondary unfavorable factor caused the Business

Curve to drop around 3½ points bringing business activity to 13 points below normal through January and February 1878 while the aspect was in effect.

In the spring of 1878, the Business Curve moved upward four points as the unfavorable secondary factors disappeared. In the fall of 1878, the favorable secondary factor, Jupiter in Aquarius in conjunction with the North Node, lifted the curve another point and one-half which brought the curve between 7 and 8 points below normal by the end of the year.

During January, February, and March 1879 the Business Curve receded four points as Neptune in Taurus was square the Node in Aquarius. This brought business activity down to 11 points below normal.

On April 13, 1879, the North Node passed out of Aquarius into the sign of Capricorn which indicated that the Business Cycle was now in a slow uptrend swing from "Below Normal" to "Normal" as is shown on the Business Cycle Chart. The normal or transition point was reached when the North Node passed into the sign of Scorpio three years later on May 19, 1882.

When the North Node moved into Capricorn in April 1879, it formed a very favorable aspect *(trine, 120 degrees)* with the powerful planet Pluto. The presence of this strong secondary factor indicated a sharp upturn in business activity and this factor carried the Business Curve from 11 points below normal to normal by August of the same year. This upturn in business was the beginning of a three year boom, known in financial history as the "Gold Resumption Prosperity Period."

The Gold Resumption Prosperity Period 1879-1883

Although the influence of the powerful secondary factor, Pluto trine the North Node, diminished in October 1879, three other favorable secondary factors were present: Uranus, Neptune and Mars trine (120 *degrees)* the North Node with Mars and Neptune

McWhirter Theory of Stock Market Forecasting

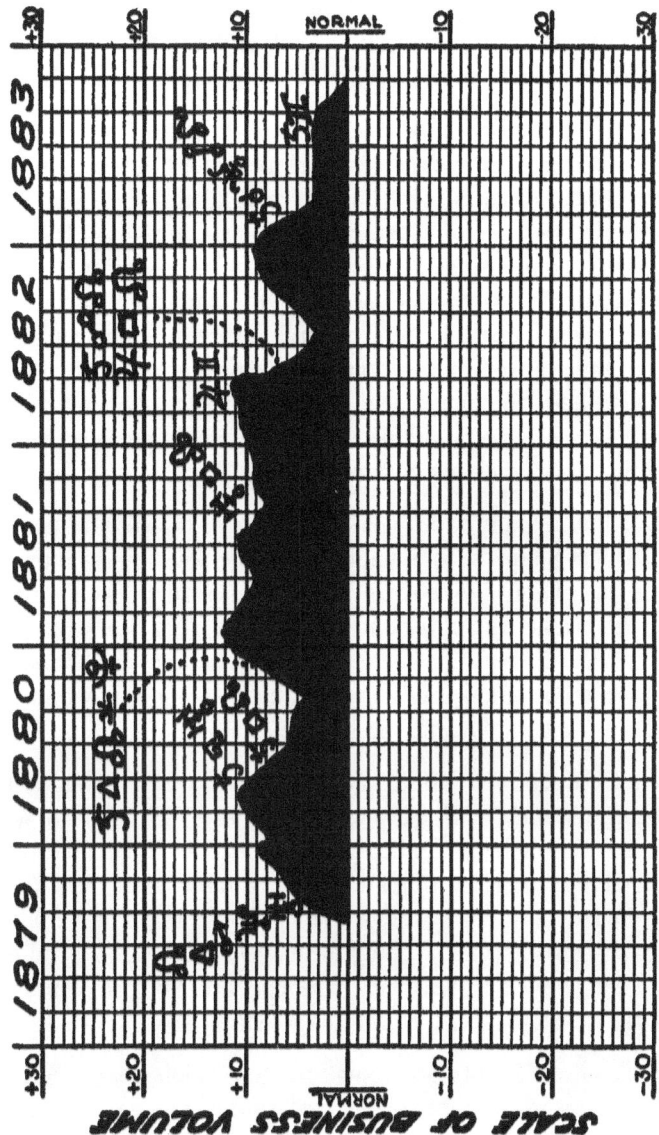

Gold Resumption Prosperity Period, 1879-1883

in conjunction with each other and in favorable aspect to Uranus. The Business Curve, as a result of this concentrative power, continued to rise through the fall of 1879 and by December stood at nine points above normal. This was a 20 point rise in business activity in nine months.

The Business Curve rose two points through January and February 1880. In March 1880, an unfavorable secondary factor, Saturn square (90 *degrees*) the North Node, came into effect. The Business Curve dropped six points through September 1880. Saturn was also in sesquiquadrate aspect to Uranus during these five months. This combination of unfavorable secondary factors would have caused a greater drop in business activity had not Uranus also been in trine aspect (120 *degrees*) to the North Node, which was a very favorable secondary factor present that kept business volume above normal.

Stock and grain prices went lower under the slightly unfavorable aspect Saturn sesquiquadrate Uranus. Saturn passed through Aries from May 1878 to April 1881. In this sign position, it passed over the Midheaven of the chart of the New York Stock Exchange and during this period affected the major trend of the Stock Market by keeping stock prices lower than they ordinarily would have been during this two and one-half year period.

On October 31, 1880, the North Node moved into Sagittarius, forming a favorable trine aspect (120 *degrees*) with Saturn, which in itself was in semi-sextile aspect (30 *degrees*) to the powerful planet Pluto. This combination of favorable secondary factors sent the Business Curve upward seven points through the fall and January 1881, at which time the Business Curve was standing at 12 points above normal. There was a decline of three points from this business prosperity high through May 1881.

In April 1881, both Saturn and Jupiter, which were in conjunction in Aries, moved into the sign of Taurus where they were still in conjunction with each other, besides being in orb of an approaching conjunction aspect with Neptune, also in Taurus, and in orb of a trine aspect (120 *degrees*) with Uranus. This was an unusual configuration of planets since five major planets were in earthy or materialistic signs. They were Jupiter, Saturn, Neptune, and Pluto in Taurus and Uranus in Virgo.

Through history and research it has been found that when several major planets are in earth signs at the same time, that men's minds turn toward the getting of material things in life and, therefore, business activity and volume increases.

Business activity stayed around 11 points above normal throughout the year of 1881. There was a two point drop in the summer and fall as Uranus was in square aspect (90 *degrees*) to the North Node. This unfavorable secondary factor would have pointed out more of a drop in the Business Curve if four major planets had not been in favorable aspect to each other while all four planets were in earth signs—three of these planets, Neptune, Saturn, and Jupiter, being in the financial sign of Taurus.

During January and February 1882, the Business Curve recovered its two point loss and the top of this rise was 11 points above normal, where the Business Curve remained through March and part of April.

On April 22, 1882, the expansive planet Jupiter moved into the sign of Gemini, the sign which has part rulership over the United States, together with the sign of Cancer. At the same time Jupiter formed a square (90 *degrees*) aspect with the North Node. This caused the curve to turn downward slightly. On May 19, 1882, the North Node moved into Scorpio, the sign on the normal point of the Business Cycle Chart. As Saturn was still in Taurus, it formed at this time an opposition (180 *degree*) aspect with the North Node which lasted through August 1882. This unfavorable secondary factor caused the Business Curve to drop six points.

Through the fall the Business Curve turned upward and regained four points of its loss by December. In January 1883, the Business Curve turned downward and marked the beginning of the long, and slow depression from 1883 to 1886, which has come to be known in history as the "Depression of 1884."

The Depression of 1884

When the North Node moved into Scorpio, May 19, 1882, the Business Cycle Chart indicated that business conditions were passing through a transition period which would last until June 22, 1885, corresponding with the time taken for the passage of the North Node through the signs of Scorpio and Libra, transition signs on the Business Cycle Chart. The normal trend of business volume following this transition period was from "normal to high" if no unfavorable secondary factors were present to distort the Curve below the normal or transition point. During the Depression of 1884, business volume decreased to 13 points below normal; therefore, one or more unfavorable secondary factors must have been present during this period.

Saturn and Neptune in conjunction in Taurus were moving in opposition (180 *degrees*) to the North Node in Scorpio in December 1882 and January 1883, and these factors precipitated the drop in the Curve which went from nine points above normal to three points above normal by the end of August.

On May 24, 1883, the price-depressing planet Saturn moved into the sign of Gemini which governs the United States. This unfavorable secondary factor always affects business conditions adversely when it transits the signs ruling the United States.

Saturn has passed through the sign of Gemini three times since 1850 and each time the United States has suffered under depressed business conditions and hard times. The Business Curve moved downward during the summer and fall of 1883 under this influence. By December the Curve was standing at four points below normal.

On December 7, 1883, the North Node moved into Libra. The Business Cycle Chart indicates that the normal position of the

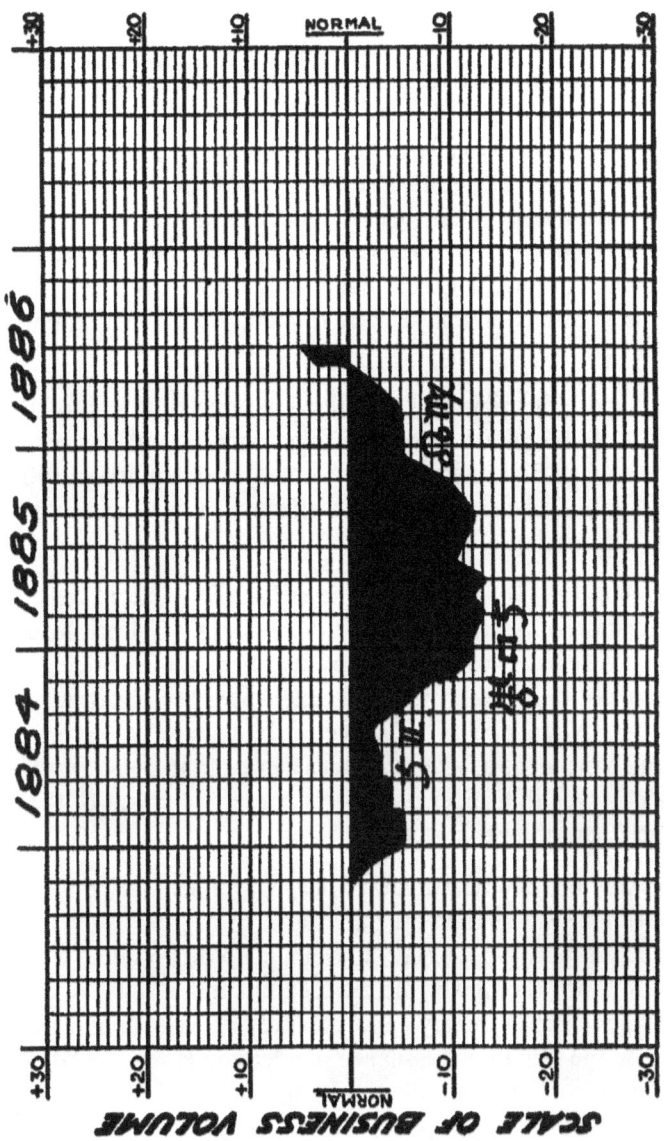

Depression of 1884

business activity Curve should be slightly above normal due to the fact the sign of Libra is slightly above Scorpio, which is the sign representing the normal point in this system of forecasting the trend of business. Favorable and unfavorable secondary factors, it has been found, can distort the curve from its logical and correct position by as much as 20 percent, depending on the strength of the secondary factor or combination of factors involved. Saturn required two and one-half years to transit a sign and its passage through Gemini should correspond with a two and one-half year period of depressed business conditions for this country. This is the case as can readily be seen by reference to the diagram of this depression.

Rail and Industrial stocks declined in price during all of 1884. Another unfavorable secondary factor came into play during the summer when Saturn in Gemini formed a square aspect (90 *degrees*) with Uranus in Virgo. The effects of this aspect were felt through the spring of 1886.

On April 30, 1884, J. R. Keene failed. This started the crash. The lunation of April 25, 1884 fell in 5 degrees Taurus in square aspect (90 *degrees*) to Mars, one of the rulers of the Midheaven of the Chart of the New York Stock Exchange. Mars was in 11 degrees Leo. When the Sun had moved to 10 degrees Taurus on April 30, which made the aspect less than a degree from being exact, and the Moon was in Cancer passing over the Ascendant of the Exchange Chart, the panic started.

On May 6, 1884, Grant and Ward, as well as Marine National Bank, failed. At this time the Sun was in 15 degrees Taurus in exact square aspect (90 *degrees*) to Mars in 15 degrees Leo with the Moon in Libra, the sign on the lowest point of the New York Stock Exchange Chart. A money panic occurred on May 12 and 13, followed on the 14th by the issuance of Clearing House Certificates. Fisk and Hatch and the Metropolitan Bank of New York failed May 15, 1884. On May 12 and 13—the days of the money panic—the Sun was in conjunction with Neptune, the other ruler of the Midheaven of the Exchange Chart, and the Sun and Neptune were in square aspect to Mars, while Mars and Neptune, the two rulers of the Midheaven of the New York Stock Exchange Chart, were in square aspect to each other while the Moon was in opposition aspect (180 *degrees)* to Saturn in Gemini. This series of unfavorable secondary factors clearly indicated the financial trouble of this period.

It is a noticeable fact that the Moon is usually in one of the angles of the New York Stock Exchange Chart when a panic or slump occurs. If the lunation indicates a change in the trend of the Stock Market for the following month, watch carefully for the days when the Moon passes through Aries, Cancer, Libra, and Capricorn. The drop usually will occur on one of these days.

During the summer and fall of 1884, the unfavorable secondary factor, Saturn in Gemini square Uranus in Virgo, was so close that business volume shrank leaving the Business Curve standing at 13 points below normal by January 1885. The force of this unfavorable aspect was felt throughout the spring and summer of 1885.

On June 25, 1885, the North Node moved into the sign of Virgo, indicating that the natural position of the Business Curve should be above normal if it were not distorted by an unfavorable secondary factor. The influence of the Saturn-Uranus square aspect began to lessen during November and December 1885, and by the end of the year the Business Curve had moved upward six points.

The Business Curve continued its climb through the spring of 1886 and by June had moved to four points above normal. This was a nine point rise in business activity in six months. This rise continued throughout the year and reached 11 points above normal by March 1887.

On January 13, 1887, the North Node moved into Leo, the sign on the high point of the Business Cycle Chart, where it remained through July 30, 1888. This indicated that business volume and activity should be at a high level, at least 10 to 15 points above normal, if there were no unfavorable secondary factors present to distort the Curve. However, Saturn and Uranus were within eight degrees of each other and moved closer through July 1887. The Business Curve correspondingly dropped from eleven to two points above normal during this period.

On August 19, 1887, Saturn moved into Leo, and for three months was within slight orb of a very favorable trine (120 *degrees*) aspect with Uranus. The Business Curve rose six points, dropping in December as Saturn and Uranus moved out of orb. At the same time the depressing planet Saturn moved within orb of a conjunction with the North Node, which governs business conditions. This immediately turned the Business Curve downward through July 1888. There was a drop in business volume from seven points above normal to two points below normal, the Business Curve turned downward nine points altogether.

The Railroad Prosperity Period 1888-1892

The North Node moved from Leo to the sign of Cancer on August 1, 1888. The Business Curve was now starting slowly downward toward the normal point which it reached in September 1891. In the interim the North Node passed through Cancer and Gemini, two signs closely related to the affairs of the United States. During the fall of 1888, the Curve rose to six points above normal as Saturn in Leo and Uranus in Libra were in favorable sextile (60 *degrees*) aspect to each other. In January 1889, Uranus turned retrograde, that is, started moving backward in its orbit. At the same time it formed an exact square aspect (90 *degrees*) with the North Node, which was unfavorable. This caused the Business Curve to drop five points through June 1889, at which time Uranus turned direct in its motion and started moving away from the North Node as the Business Curve stood at only one point above normal.

The Curve moved up sharply through the summer and fall of 1889 as Saturn in Leo was in close sextile (60 *degrees)* aspect with Uranus in Libra. The powerful planet Pluto was in conjunction

McWhirter Theory of Stock Market Forecasting

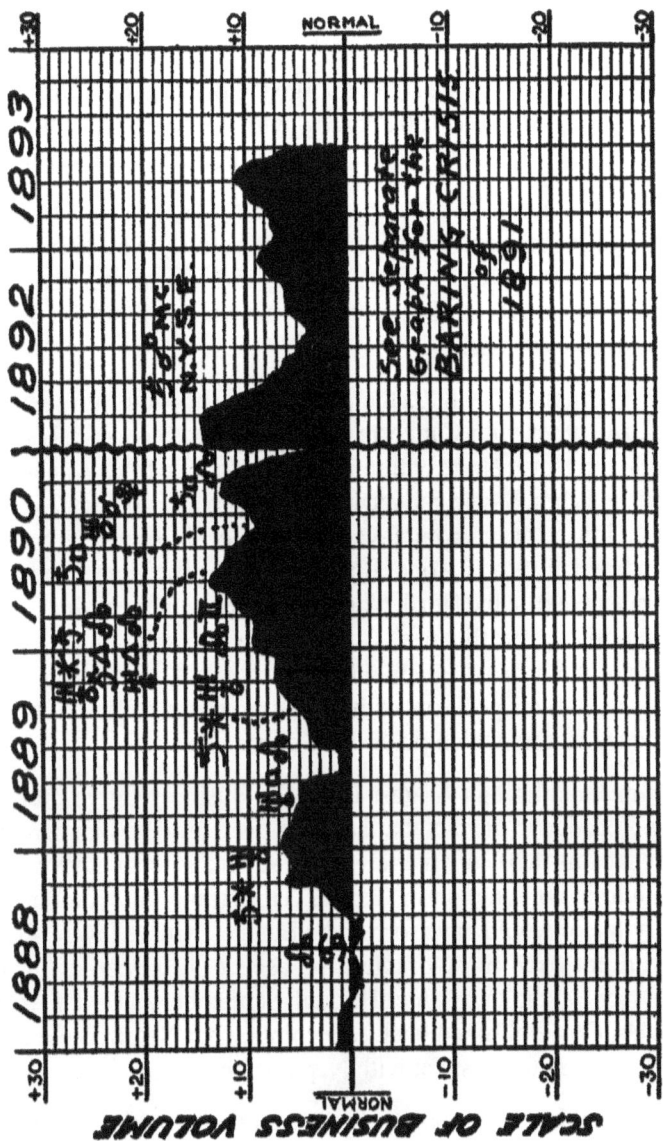

Railroad Prosperity Period, 1888-1892

with Neptune, one of the New York Stock Exchange planetary rulers.

Saturn moved into the sign of Virgo October 7, 1889, forming a favorable sextile aspect (60 *degrees)* with the North Node through December. At the end of the year the Business Curve stood at nine points above normal.

The year 1890 opened with business activity well above normal. The Business Curve from January to May moved from nine points above normal to 14 points above normal, a total rise of five points in five months.

On February 19, 1890, the North Node moved into Gemini, which (together with Cancer) rules the United States. This move brought the North Node within orb of a favorable trine aspect with Uranus in Libra. Saturn moved back into Leo on February 25. This brought into effect a strong favorable relationship between Saturn, Uranus, and the North Node. Uranus was trine the North Node and Saturn was sextile the North Node, while being in favorable aspect to each other. The Business Curve, therefore, stood at 13 points above normal in May. It would have been only slightly above normal in its natural position without the presence of the favorable secondary factors which pushed the curve upward.

From June through August 1890, the Business Curve dropped four points due to the fact that Saturn moved into the sign of Virgo where it came in orb of an unfavorable square aspect with Neptune and Pluto in conjunction in Gemini. This strong unfavorable secondary factor would have forced the Business Curve lower if Uranus had not been in favorable trine aspect (120 *degrees)* to the North Node at the same time. Through September and October, the Business Curve climbed back two points when Saturn moved out of orb of the square aspect with Neptune and Pluto.

In November 1890, Saturn formed an unfavorable aspect with the North Node. This unfavorable factor pointed out the business crisis which lasted through June 1891, and which is known in financial history as the "Baring Crisis." This crisis was precipitated in England by the failure of Baring Brothers. The Business Curve dropped from 12 points above normal to seven points below normal—a total drop of 19 points in six months.

Baring Crisis—1891

Stock prices declined sharply during this period and commodity prices were the lowest since the War Between the States.

In May 1891, the Business Curve moved sharply upward as the North Node and Saturn moved out of orb of the unfavorable square aspect between them.

From January to the end of June 1891, Saturn in Virgo formed a slightly unfavorable aspect with Uranus. This semi-square aspect (45 *degrees)* added weight to the unfavorable aspect between Saturn and the North Node in force at the time of the Baring Crisis.

Since the powerful planet Pluto was in conjunction with Neptune, co-ruler of the Midheaven of the New York Stock Exchange, and the North Node, the Business Curve turned sharply upward in May and reached 13 points above normal, a level which it maintained through October. A drop of two points in the Business Curve occurred in November due to the fact that the North Node no longer was in conjunction with Pluto and Neptune.

The North Node moved into Taurus on September 10, 1891. Since Taurus is the sign on the normal or transition point of the Business Cycle Chart, the movement of the North Node into Taurus indicated a change in the Business Curve for several years to come. The primary or major cycle of business was in a transition period lasting until March 28, 1893, when the North Node moved into Aries, indicating that the trend of the Business Curve was moving from normal to low and that the business cycle was moving downward for four years until the North Node moved out of the sign of Aquarius on November 22, 1897. Aquarius is the low point on the Business Cycle Chart and the Business Curve did not

Business Cycles and Stock Market Trends 1850-1950

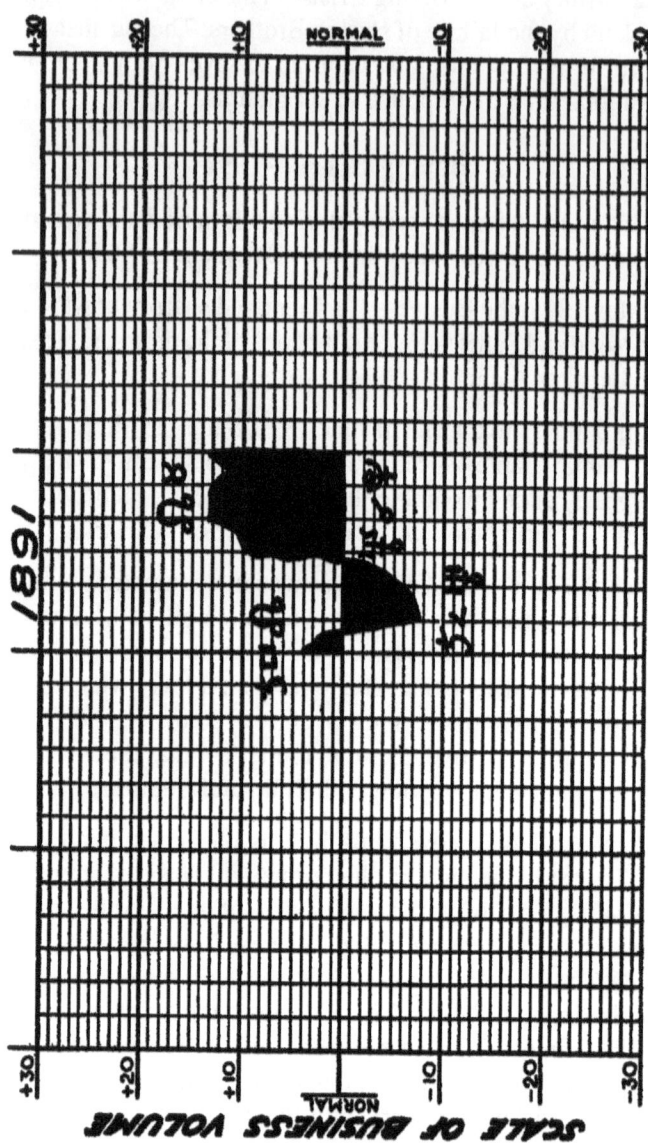

Baring Crisis, 1891

start upward until after that point had been reached. The North Node passed through Aquarius from May 4, 1896 to November 22, 1897.

On October 22, 1891, the fiery planet Mars moved into the sign of Libra where it remained through December 7 of the same year. Libra is the sign on the fourth or lowest angle of the New York Stock Exchange Chart and also a transition sign on the Business Cycle Chart; therefore, it is particularly sensitive to planetary transits. Mars usually depresses the Curve slightly as it passes through Libra; in this case the Curve dropped two points.

The Curve turned upward three points through December 1891, and January 1892, reaching a high in February of 14 points above normal.

From March until August 1892, Saturn in Virgo moved in opposition aspect to the Midheaven of the New York Stock Exchange in 28 degrees Pisces. This caused an 11 point drop in the Business Curve during this period, which marked the end of the Railroad Prosperity Period.

There was a recovery of five points through the fall of 1892 from the low point of August which had carried business activity to two points above normal. In December the Business Curve stood at eight points above normal. This was due to the slightly favorable semi-sextile aspect (30 *degrees)* between Saturn in Libra and Uranus in Scorpio. Stock Market prices rose under this favorable influence. Business activity dropped one point during January and February of 1893, but the Business Curve rose three points through April, reaching a high of 10 points above normal, which was the top level reached before the Panic of 1893.

The Panic of 1893-1895

This financial crisis in the United States was precipitated in May by the failure of the Chemical National Bank of Chicago and others, including The National Cordage Company. The Business

Business Cycles and Stock Market Trends 1850-1950

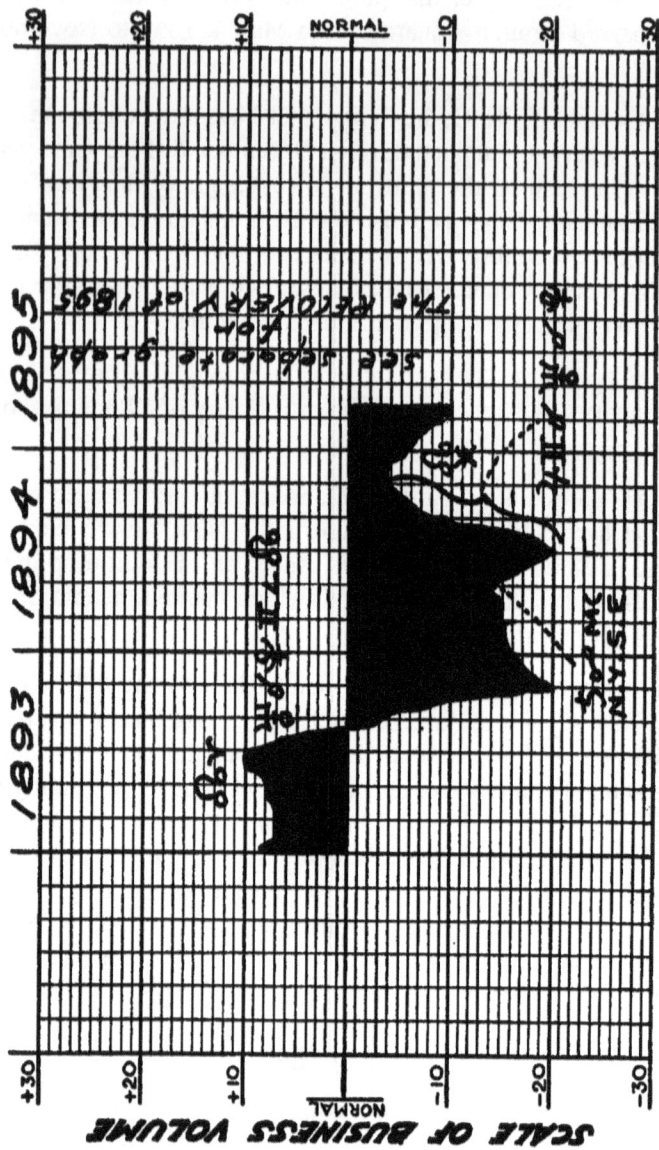

Panic of 1893-1895

Curve plummeted from 10 points above normal to 20 points below normal. This was a drop of 30 points in business activity from May to August 1893. Stocks dropped sharply in value, especially Industrials, which were off as much as 30 points in the Industrial Averages.

The sharp and irregular depression of 1893 came at a time when prices were the lowest they had ever been in the economic history of this country. Crop failures both in 1893 and 1894 were numerous.

The North Node was in 28 degrees Aries and moving backward over the Midheaven of the New York Stock Exchange during May 1893. Pluto and Neptune were in conjunction in Gemini, the sign which is co-significator of the United States, and together they were forming an unfavorable semi-square aspect (45 *degrees)* to the North Node. These secondary factors indicated the financial crisis affecting this country during this period. The Business Cycle Curve had started downward and the unfavorable secondary factors present depressed the curve 20 percent. *(All secondary factors, favorable or unfavorable, have the power to inflate or deflate the normal trend of the Business Curve from 1 to 20 percent depending upon the strength of the secondary factor involved.)*

Any planet *(or the Nodes which in this method of forecasting have the strength of planets and are considered as such)* which passes over the Midheaven or tenth angle of the New York Stock Exchange Chart *always* indicates in advance a coming definite change in trend of Stock Market prices; and if the planet is unfavorable, it indicates a financial panic or business crisis. These warning signals are always given months in advance. Any trader buying and selling on these signals is the master of economic law instead of its victim.

From September 1893 to April 1894, the Business Curve rose from 20 points below normal to 14 points below normal. This was a total of six points rise as the unfavorable semi-square aspect (45 *degrees)* between the North Node in Aries and Pluto and Neptune in Gemini moved into a favorable sextile (60 *degrees*) angle. In April 1894, the Business Curve dropped to 20 points below normal. Saturn at this time was in 22 degrees Libra in opposition aspect (180 *degrees*) to the Midheaven of the New York Stock Exchange Chart. The lunation for April 1894 fell in 16 degrees Aries in the Midheaven of the Chart in opposition (180 *degrees*) to Saturn. This unfavorable secondary influence caused stock prices to drop sharply.

In May 1894, the lunation fell in 14 degrees Taurus in opposition (180 *degrees*) aspect to Uranus. The adverse affect of this lunation kept the Business Curve down through May.

On June 3, 1894, the lunation fell in 12 degrees Gemini in conjunction with Neptune, Pluto, and Jupiter and in square aspect (90 *degrees*) with Mars, the co-ruler of the Midheaven of the New York Stock Exchange Chart. This unfavorable aspect of Mars kept stock prices down as well as general business conditions; however, recovery factors were at work and when the temporary effects of this lunation (28 *days*) were over the Business Curve took a sharp turn upward. This was due to the presence of the expansive planet Jupiter in conjunction with the powerful planets Pluto and Neptune in the sign of Gemini, which strongly influences the United States. Stocks and bonds rose under these favorable secondary factors and Industrial Averages had approximately a 20 point rise in a year's time.

From July through December 1894, the Business Curve rose sharply to five points below normal. This was a 15 percent increase in business activity during this period and preceded the period known in history as "The Recovery of 1895."

The Recovery of 1895

On October 16, 1894, the North Node moved into Pisces and reference to the Business Cycle Chart shows that the *normal* trend of the Curve was slowly moving lower. The powerful secondary factor, Pluto in conjunction with Neptune in the sign of Gemini,

McWhirter Theory of Stock Market Forecasting

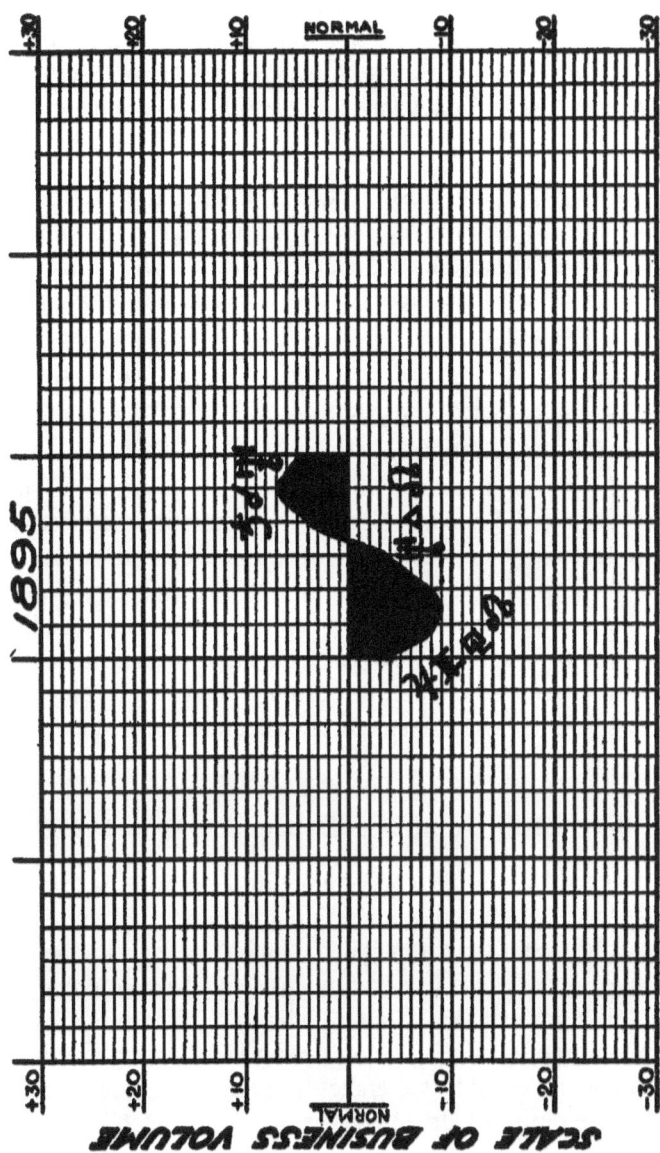

Recovery of 1895

which rules the United States, moved the Business Curve upward to nearly four points below normal. Jupiter was also in Cancer during the fall *(Cancer is the other sign of the zodiac which with Gemini rules the United States)*, and Jupiter in this position aids rising prices.

In January 1895, the Business Curve dropped five points due to the fact that Jupiter moved back into the sign of Gemini and formed an unfavorable square aspect (90 *degrees*) with the North Node. This aspect held the Business Curve down through April when Jupiter moved out of Gemini and into Cancer again.

In April 1895, the Business Curve started upward on a 19 point rise which reached six points above normal by September as Uranus was in a favorable trine aspect (120 *degrees*) to the North Node. The North Node came into an unfavorable square (90 *degrees*) aspect with Pluto and Neptune in September and these unfavorable secondary factors stopped the rise and caused the Business Curve to drop slightly through the fall. In the meantime the price-depressing planet Saturn moved to an unfavorable conjunction aspect with the powerful governmental planet Uranus. This aspect became close enough to become effective in January and February 1896, which marked the beginning of the "Silver Campaign Depression."

The Silver Campaign Depression 1896-1897

Saturn and Uranus were in conjunction aspect during this entire depression. The nomination of William Jennings Bryan, Democrat, and the free silver campaign, did much toward bringing about this panic, as there was fear that the gold standard would be abolished. It is significant that Jupiter *(ruler of the Nation's finances)*, was in Leo *(the sign ruling Gold)* during 1896. This planetary position alone indicated an adherence to the gold standard which resulted in the defeat of Bryan and the election of McKinley.

Rails suffered a drastic decline in this depression while Industrial averages reached the lowest point since the War between the

McWhirter Theory of Stock Market Forecasting

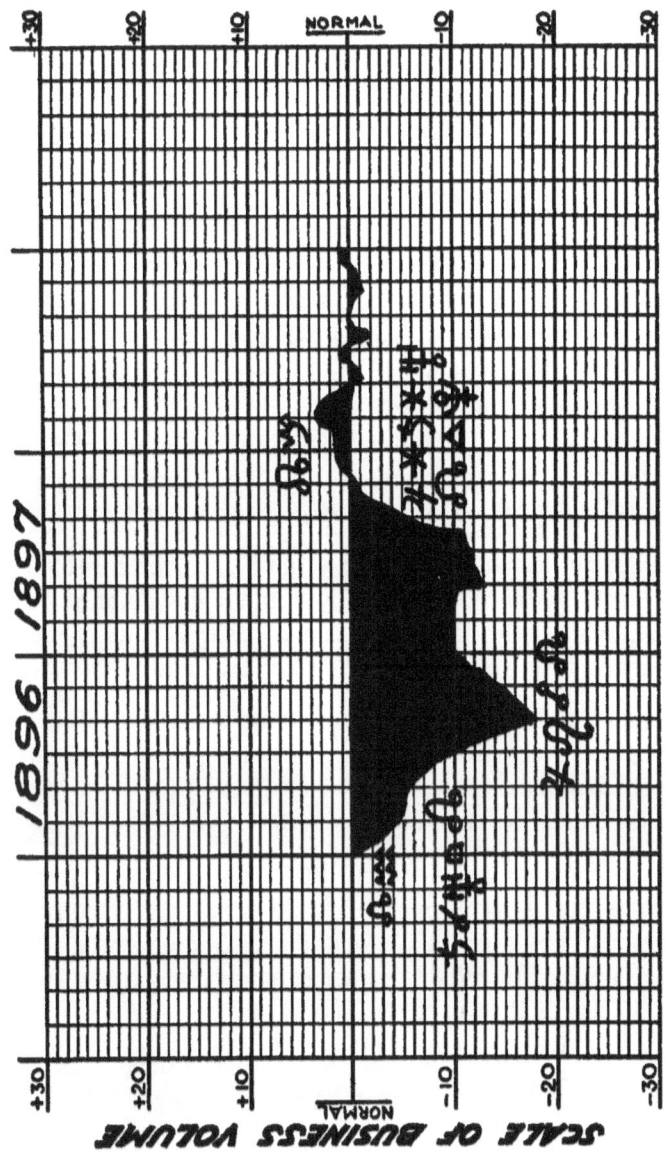

Silver Campaign Depression, 1896-1897

States. Also during this year (1896) crops were poor and commodity prices stood at the lowest point since 1869.

On May 4, 1896, the North Node moved into Aquarius, the sign on the "Low" angle of the Business Cycle Chart where it remained until November 22, 1897. The passage of the North Node through Aquarius marked the end of the downward trend of the Business Curve and the Business Cycle began slowly to swing upward from the Low Point to Normal.

When the North Node moved into Aquarius it slowly approached an unfavorable square aspect (90 *degrees*) with Uranus and Saturn in conjunction in Scorpio. This unfavorable secondary factor combined with Uranus' and Saturn's unfavorable influence, depressed the Curve 18 points. Jupiter in Leo was also in an unfavorable square aspect (90 *degrees*) to Uranus and Saturn; and in unfavorable opposition aspect (180 *degrees*) to the North Node.

Jupiter moved out of Leo into Virgo September 28, 1896, and this transit lifted the Curve slightly from the low point of August and September when stock prices and business activity reached their lowest level since the War between the States.

Neptune and the powerful planet Pluto in Gemini, although 7 degrees apart, were in orb of a conjunction aspect and this powerful secondary factor, in the sign which co-rules the United States, lifted the Business Curve 6 points by January 1897.

During January and February 1897, the Business Curve rose two more points where it stood at 10 points below normal. In March 1897, however, the Curve dropped back to 12 points below normal as Saturn turned Retrograde in motion, which was a retarding influence on the Curve.

In April and May 1897, the North Node formed a favorable trine aspect (120 *degrees*) with the powerful planet Pluto. This aspect lifted the Business Curve slightly which became a sharp upturn in August when the expansive planet Jupiter moved in sextile aspect (60 *degrees*) to Saturn and Uranus in conjunction in Scorpio. This combination of secondary factors exerted a favorable influence which caused the Curve to rise six points in August, and by the end of October the Curve stood at two points below the normal line.

On November 22, 1897, the North Node passed out of Aquarius, the sign on the low point of the Business Cycle Chart, into the sign of Capricorn. The Business Curve was now on a slow long swing upward from low to normal business activity. As the Node moved into Capricorn it formed a favorable 60 degree angle with Uranus in Scorpio and this favorable secondary factor took the Business Curve three points above normal through February 1898. Jupiter was also in conjunction with the North Node during January and February 1898.

During all of 1898 the Business Curve remained dose to the normal line. In May the Curve was 1 point below normal; in June, 1 point above normal; in July, 2 points below normal; in October, 1 point below normal; and in December, 1 point above normal. Although the normal position of the Business Curve was below normal, the fact that Jupiter was in a favorable 60 degree angle (sextile aspect) with both Saturn and Uranus, this secondary factor lifted the Curve to the normal point during 1898.

During 1899 the Business Curve rose steadily from 1 point above normal to 11 points above normal at the end of the year. This was due to the favorable aspect between Jupiter and Uranus to the North Node. Jupiter and Uranus were in a 30 degree angle (semi-sextile aspect) to each other, Uranus was in semi-sextile (30 *degrees)* aspect to the North Node and Jupiter was in a favorable sextile aspect (60 *degrees)* to the North Node. These aspects lasted through June when the North Node moved out of Capricorn into Sagittarius on June 10, 1899.

The passage of the North Node into Sagittarius took the natural position of the Business Curve to nearly normal. The strong secondary factors present pushed the Curve above normal during the year.

When the North Node moved into Sagittarius, it was within 10 degrees of a conjunction aspect with the depressing planet Saturn. This aspect usually depresses the Business Curve temporarily, but Jupiter in a favorable 30 degree angle to both Saturn and the Node at this time sent the Curve upward instead, through January and February 1900. This sharp upward trend in the latter part of 1899 was the forerunner of the three-year period of above-normal prices known in history as the "Merger Prosperity Period."

The Merger Prosperity Period 1900-1903

Business activity started strong at the beginning of 1900, but soon slumped well below the normal line. This was due to the fact that the North Node came into an unfavorable 180 degree angle *(opposition aspect)* with the powerful planet Pluto. Uranus and Jupiter in conjunction in Sagittarius were also forming a conjunction aspect with the North Node. From March through November Pluto was in opposition to the North Node, Uranus, and Jupiter. The Business Curve dropped from 11 points above normal to 5 points below normal under this combination of unfavorable secondary factors.

In December 1900, two astronomical changes came about which turned the Business Curve upward. The North Node moved into Scorpio on December 31, 1900, and Saturn moved into orb of a favorable 30 degree angle with Uranus.

When the North Node moved into Scorpio the Curve of business activity had reached the normal point, inasmuch as Scorpio is the sign on the normal point of the Business Cycle Chart. Without the presence of secondary factors to distort the Curve up or down, business activity was now standing at normal. The Curve rose to 5 points above normal by April, 1901, which was due to the presence of the favorable semi-sextile aspect between Saturn and Uranus. This aspect lasted all year. Commodity prices rose as well as Rail stocks during the year.

During January and February 1902, the Business Curve

McWhirter Theory of Stock Market Forecasting

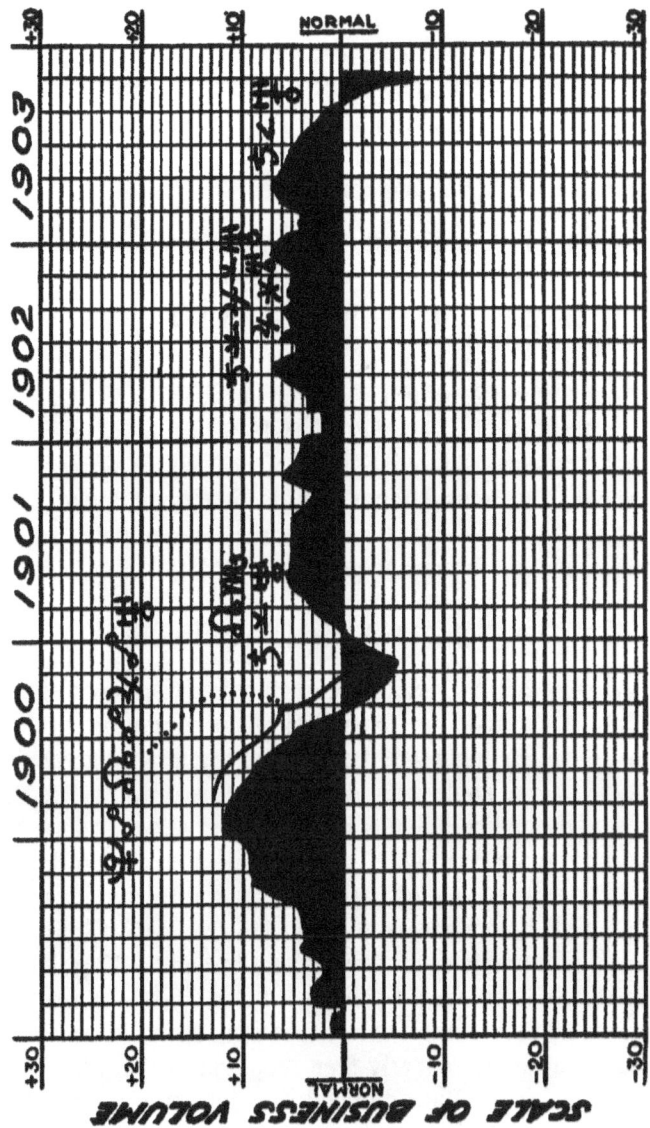

Merger Prosperity Period, 1900-1903

dropped to 2 points above normal as Jupiter formed an unfavorable 90 degree angle *(square aspect)* with the North Node. In April the effect of this aspect passed away and the Business Curve moved up three points. The Business Curve stayed between 4 and 5 points above normal during all of 1902. Saturn was in a favorable 30 degree angle to both Uranus and Jupiter and the latter was in a favorable 60 degree angle to Uranus.

On July 19, 1902, the North Node moved into Libra, which indicated that the natural position of the Business Curve, without the presence of favorable or unfavorable secondary factors, was now slightly above normal.

In the fall of 1902, Saturn was in an unfavorable 90 degree angle to the North Node. This secondary factor would have caused a drop in the Business Curve if Saturn had not been in a favorable 30 degree angle to Uranus. Uranus was also in a favorable 60 degree angle to the North Node at the same time. These factors kept the Business Curve up through the spring of 1903.

The Rich Man's Panic—1903-1904

On January 20, 1903, Saturn moved out of Capricorn and into the sign of Aquarius. This transit took Saturn out of orb of the favorable 30 degree angle with Uranus and brought it into an unfavorable 45 degree angle with Uranus the first of May. The Business Curve dropped six points by September at which time Neptune formed an unfavorable 90 degree angle with the North Node. This unfavorable secondary factor caused the Business Curve to drop 11 points below normal through January 1904. This combination of unfavorable secondary factors brought a 17 point total drop in the Business Curve causing what is known as the "Rich Man's Panic." Stocks had a correspondingly sharp drop also, with Rails suffering more severely than Industrials. According to the Dow-Jones averages, Rails dropped 18 points from 110 to 92, and Industrials dropped 17 points from 64 to 47.

On February 7, 1904, the North Node moved into Virgo, indi-

McWhirter Theory of Stock Market Forecasting

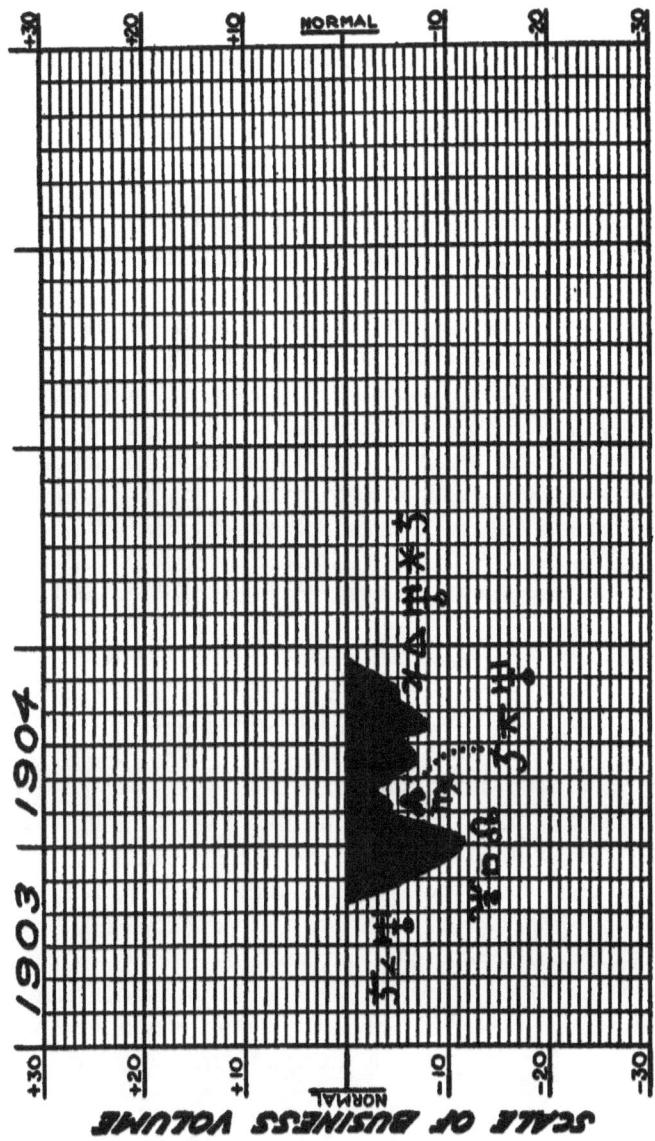

Rich Man's Panic, 1903-1904

cating that the Normal position of the Business Curve was almost to the high point on the Business Cycle Chart. The Curve rose six points during February under this influence, but dropped 4 points in May as Saturn formed an unfavorable 150 degree angle with the North Node. This influence was also felt in August 1904, when the Business Curve stood at 5 points below normal.

In September 1904, the Business Curve took a sharp upturn due to the fact that the North Node moved out of orb of aspects with Saturn and Uranus. Jupiter was in a favorable 120 degree angle with Uranus; and Saturn was within orb to form a favorable 60 degree angle with both planets. These angles were in force during the fall and by the end of December 1904, the Business Curve had risen 9 points. This recovery from the "Rich Man's Panic" marked the beginning of a three year period with above-normal business volume and rising stock market prices which has come to be known in history as the "Corporate Prosperity Period."

The Corporate Prosperity Period 1905-1907

The Business Curve was three points above normal by January 1905 and rose six more points through June of the same year. This was due to the favorable sextile (60 *degree*) angle between Saturn and Uranus. Uranus and Saturn were also in favorable aspect to the North Node at the same time. Uranus was forming a trine (120 *degrees*) angle to the North Node and Saturn was forming a sextile (60 *degrees*) angle to the North Node. Three planets in favorable aspect to each other or two planets and the North Node in mutual favorable aspect to each other are always accompanied by increased business volume and rising stock market prices. This is especially true if the planets involved are Saturn, Uranus, and Jupiter. Of course, unfavorable secondary factors present can modify these indications, but generally the upward trend prevails.

Saturn, Uranus, and the North Node were in mutual favorable relationship to each other through June 1905, and the Business Curve rose to 9 points above normal.

McWhirter Theory of Stock Market Forecasting

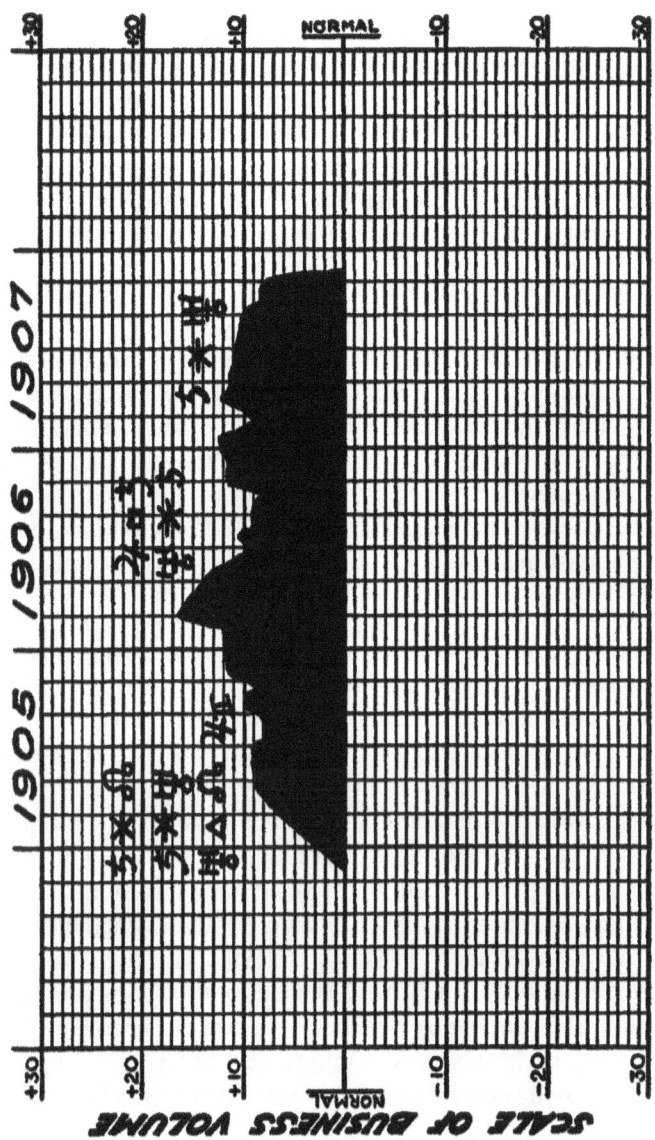

Corporate Prosperity Period, 1905-1907

On July 21, 1905, Jupiter moved Into Gemini, the sign which is co-ruler of the United States. This was a favorable secondary factor for bullish business and Stock Market activity, but it happened that at the same time that Jupiter moved into Gemini, it formed an unfavorable square (90 *degrees*) angle with Saturn and the North Node. This caused the Business Curve to drop one point; however, this was soon recovered as the North Node moved into Leo, August 25, 1905.

Leo is the sign on the highest point of the Business Cycle Chart and the passage of the North Node into the sign of Leo indicated that business volume for a year and one-half in advance would be at its Zenith with the normal position of the Business Curve sharply above normal. The Business Curve rose from 9 points above normal to 13 points above normal through January 1906. Besides the elevated Node position, two favorable secondary factors were present. Jupiter was in Gemini and Saturn was in favorable relationship to Uranus, forming a sextile or 60 degree angle.

Saturn was forming a 90 degree angle *(square aspect)* to Jupiter during the spring and summer of 1906. This caused a gradual decline of four points in the Business Curve; however, in the fall, the Business Curve recovered three points as Jupiter moved into Cancer, one of the signs which has strong affinity for the United States. During this time Saturn was in a 60 degree angle to Uranus and 120 degree angle to Jupiter, both of which were favorable aspects. In January 1907, the Business Curve receded to nine points above normal as Jupiter moved out of orb of aspect with Saturn and Uranus. These three points were recovered in March when the North Node moved into Cancer on March 16, 1907. This high was maintained until June 1907, when the Business Curve showed signs of weakness. This was due to the fact that Saturn had moved to 24 degrees Pisces in May and was forming a very unfavorable angle (90 *degrees)* with the powerful planet Pluto which was in Gemini, one of the signs so strongly influencing the United States. Saturn, in 24 degrees Pisces, had reached the sensitive degree area (*24 degrees to 28 degrees Pisces*) on the Midheaven of the Chart of the New

York Stock Exchange and clearly sounded a warning signal that the Corporate Prosperity Period was at an end and a drop in the Business Curve was imminent.

The Panic of 1907

According to this theory of forecasting business conditions together with the rise and fall of Stock Market prices, all slumps, depressions, crashes, and recessions are pointed out months in advance. The warning signals are given plainly enough and the Panic of 1907 was no exception to this rule. Anyone familiar with this theory knows that the position of Saturn on the Midheaven of the New York Stock Exchange Chart is a danger signal, and market traders should sell and sell quick before the crash comes. Saturn was in the sensitive degree (*24 degrees to 28 degrees Pisces*) from May to October 1907.

The lunation of October 7, 1907, occurred in 13 degrees Libra in square aspect (*unfavorable 90 degree angle*) to Neptune, (*one of the rulers of the Midheaven of the New York Stock Exchange*), in square aspect to Uranus and in square aspect to the North Node.

Neptune at the same time was in the sensitive degree area (*14 degrees to 17 degrees Cancer*) of the Ascendant of the New York Stock Exchange Chart. This was a double indication of trouble for business and the Stock Market. The Business Curve dropped from 8 points above normal to 18 points below normal. This was a sharp drop of 26 points in all for the Business Curve. Stocks, bonds, industrial activity and business, in general, slumped. Saturn during this period was also in unfavorable square aspect to Pluto which was in the sign of Gemini.

The Business Curve remained at 18 points below normal through May 1908. From June through December 1908, the Business Curve rose slowly 10 points due to the fact that Jupiter was trine Saturn and this tended to lessen the influence of the bad square aspect (90 *degrees)* between Saturn and Uranus.

Business Cycles and Stock Market Trends 1850-1950

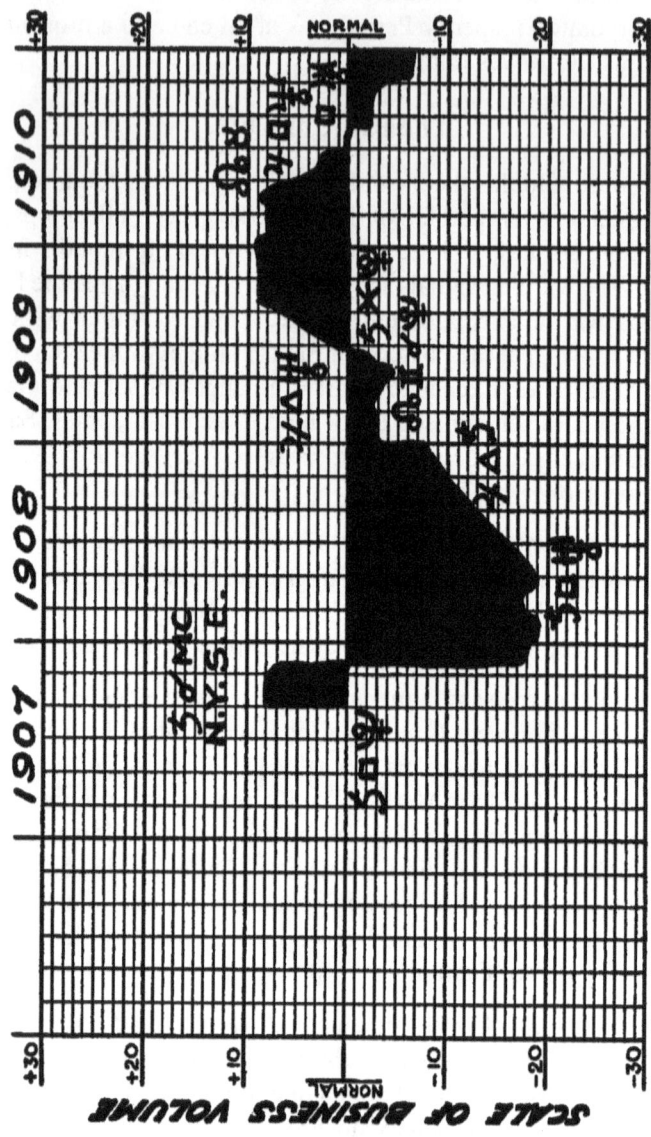

Panic of 1907

The Business Curve continued to rise in 1909 as the North Node had moved on October 1, 1908, into Gemini, the sign so strongly influencing the United States. In this position the Node came into conjunction with the powerful planet Pluto during the first half of the year. In the summer of 1909, Jupiter formed a favorable 120 degree angle with Uranus and at the same time Saturn formed a favorable 60 degree angle with Pluto. The combined influence of these two favorable secondary factors took the Business Curve upward 13 points. By December 1909, the Business Curve was 9 points above normal. The Business Curve did not hold to this level long, however, for in January 1910, Saturn, Jupiter and Uranus were all in unfavorable aspect to each other. Saturn and Jupiter were square Uranus while Saturn and Jupiter were in unfavorable opposition aspect (180 *degrees)*. The Business Curve began to drop during the remainder of 1910 and reached its low of 8 points below normal in July 1911. This was caused to a great extent by the Sherman Anti-Trust Act, which broke up large trusts and led to the depression period of 1910-1911.

On April 19, 1910, the North Node entered the sign of Taurus. This indicated that Business activity had reached a transition period which would last approximately two years, or the time it would take for the North Node to pass through the signs of Taurus and Aries. It further indicated that the trend of the Business Curve would be downward for at least five years to come unless the presence of favorable secondary factors reversed the trend temporarily during this period. *(See Business Cycle Chart.)* This was a warning signal given in April 1910 of a change in the long-term or primary trend of business activity in general, and market traders should have taken their profits and gotten out of the market at once. The same law of action and reaction which had brought the tide in was now taking the tide out. In other words, the same law of force which took the Business Cycle upward was now taking the Cycle downward—action and reaction being equal. The technical position of the Business Curve was around normal while the North Node transited Taurus, and slightly below normal as the North

Node passed through the position of Aries.

During the fall of 1910, Jupiter was forming a 90 degree angle or square aspect with both Uranus and Neptune. This unfavorable secondary factor depressed the Business Curve six points by the end of the year.

During the first six months of 1911 the Business Curve dropped 2 more points as Saturn and Uranus were in orb of a square aspect again and Jupiter was in opposition aspect (180 *degrees)* to Saturn.

In July 1911, Saturn came within orb of a trine aspect (120 *degrees)* with Uranus. This very favorable secondary factor lifted the Business Curve three points through December 1911, even though the North Node passed into Aries November 10, 1911, indicating that the "normal" or technical position of the Business Curve was below normal now.

The first six months of 1912, Jupiter was in Sagittarius and in favorable aspect to the North Node and Uranus. This lifted the Business Curve five points above normal. In July 1912, Saturn moved into Gemini and formed a favorable trine (120 *degrees*) aspect with Uranus. This lifted the Business Curve 3 more points above normal. The high was reached in January and February 1913, when the Business Curve stood at 9 points above normal. After this time the Business Curve went down through the remainder of 1913, bringing about what is known in history as the "War Depression" period.

The War Depression 1913-1914

Jupiter moved into Capricorn in January 1913, and at the same time formed an unfavorable square aspect (90 *degrees)* with the North Node. Since the technically correct position of the Business Curve was below the normal line, the Business Curve began to recede during the remainder of 1913.

The North Node moved into Pisces May 28, 1913. This indicated a technically lower position for the Business Curve.

McWhirter Theory of Stock Market Forecasting

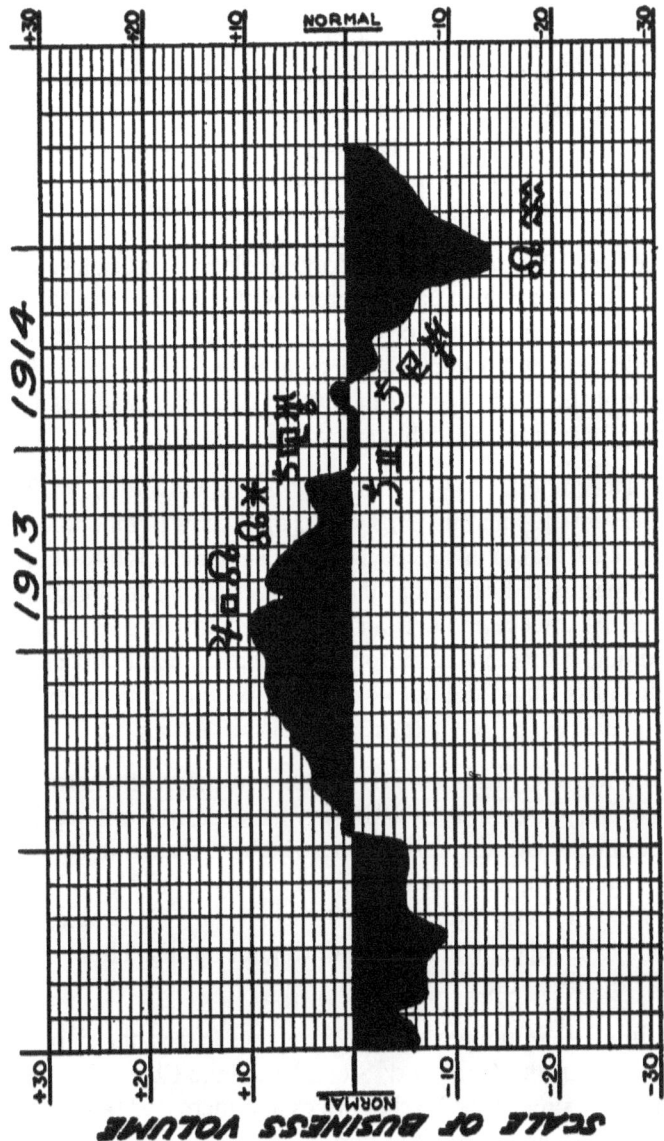

War Depression, 1913-1914

In September 1913, Saturn formed a slightly unfavorable aspect with Uranus (*sesquiquadrate of* 135 *degrees*) which lasted through May 1915. This was further accentuated by the fact that Saturn was in Gemini, the sign which has a strong influence over the United States. Up until 1913 this secondary factor was neutralized by the fact that Saturn was in favorable aspect to Uranus. When this aspect passed, the influence of Saturn in Gemini was felt.

The year 1914 saw the New York Stock Exchange closed from July to December due to the outbreak of the World War. Business was poor and commodity prices were extremely low. Liquidation of stocks held by European buyers was mainly responsible for the closing of the Exchange. At the end of 1914 the Business Curve stood at 14 points below the normal line.

On December 19, 1914, the North Node moved out of Pisces into the sign of Aquarius. This sign is on the low point of the Business Cycle Chart in this theory, and the passage of the North Node into Aquarius indicated that the Business Curve technically had reached its lowest point. It also indicated that business activity would not be this low again for many years to come. In actuality, the Business Curve did not go below this point until seven years later in 1921.

Although the Business Curve remained below the normal line for the first six months of 1915, it was steadily climbing during this period toward the normal line which it reached in July. This rise began as Jupiter was in conjunction with the North Node in trine (120 *degrees)* aspect with Saturn. Saturn also came within orb of a trine aspect with Uranus during the spring. These secondary factors lifted the Curve sharply.

In July 1915, Jupiter reached 28 degrees Pisces, the sign on the Midheaven of the New York Stock Exchange Chart. This transit pointed to rising Stock Market prices and increased business volume which marked the latter part of 1915, all of 1916 and 1917, and part of 1918. This was the beginning of the period known in economic history as the "War Prosperity" period.

War Prosperity—1915-1918

From July through December 1915, the Business Curve rose 13 points above the normal line. This was a rise of 27 points in all for the Business Curve or business volume for the year. During the last six months of 1915, Uranus was in conjunction with the North Node, and Jupiter was in a favorable semi-sextile aspect to both Uranus and the North Node.

During all of 1916, the Business Curve remained between 13 and 16 points above normal. On July 4, 1916, the North Node passed into Capricorn, which lifted the technical position of the Business Curve slightly, although its "Normal" position was still under the normal line. Favorable secondary factors, however, lifted the Business Curve to its above normal position during this period. Jupiter was in Aries during most of this year and therefore was passing over the Midheaven of the New York Stock Exchange Chart. This was an indication of booming industrial activity. Jupiter's transit over this point every 12 years has usually marked a prosperity period in business activity or the beginning of such a period in financial and economic history.

The first half of 1917 was marked by a continuation of the high business volume of 1916 and the Business Curve remained around 14 points above normal. On June 30, 1917, Jupiter moved into Gemini, the sign which is co-ruler of the United States. In December 1917, Saturn came within orb of an unfavorable opposition aspect (180 *degrees)* with Uranus. This brought about a 5 point drop in the Business Curve which was followed by a decrease of 2 more points in January and February 1918. These two planets moved out of orb until August 1918. The presence of this unfavorable secondary factor the last half of 1918 would have taken the Business Curve down sharply if it had not been for the fact that the North Node was in Sagittarius where it had been since January 22, 1918. In this position the North Node was in favorable aspect to both Saturn and Uranus. This mitigated the influence of the unfavorable Saturn-Uranus aspect to a great extent.

Business Cycles and Stock Market Trends 1850-1950

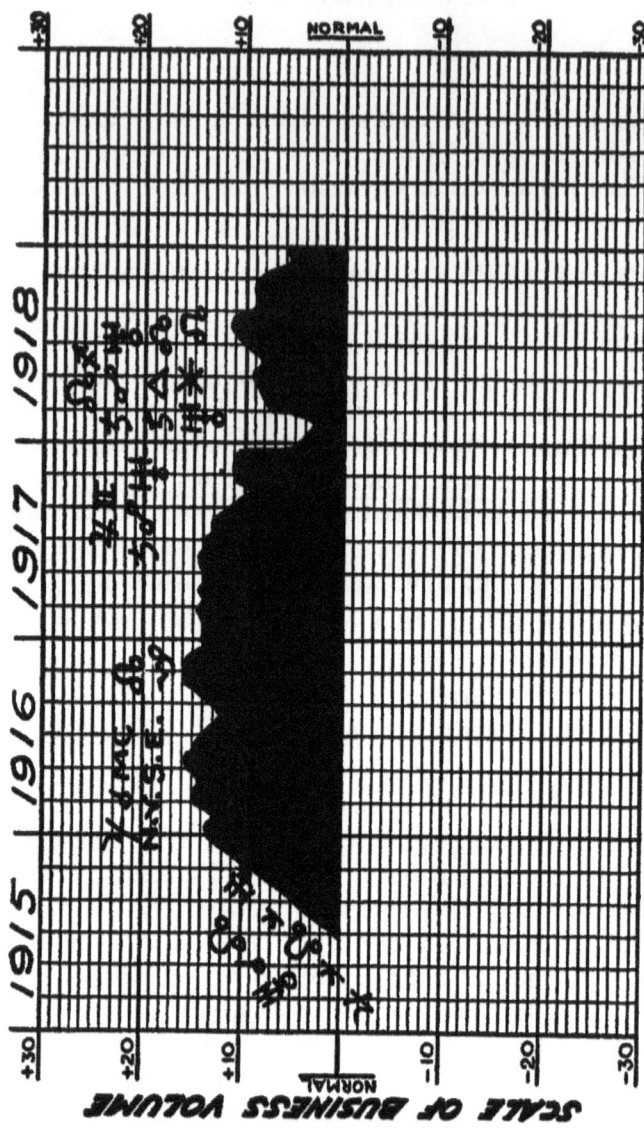

War Prosperity Period, 1915-1918

The effect of the unfavorable Saturn-Uranus aspect was felt during the first six months of 1919, when the Business Curve dropped to 8 points below normal. There was a temporary upturn during July and August 1919, when Uranus formed a favorable trine aspect (120 *degrees*) with Pluto. This favorable secondary factor lifted the Curve to 7 points above normal.

The North Node passed out of Sagittarius into Scorpio August 10, 1919, lifting the technical position of the Business Curve to the normal line. Scorpio is one of the transition points on the Business Cycle Chart. As the North Node passes through Scorpio and Libra it marks a two year transition period when the Curve starts its five-year trend from normal to high on the Business Cycle Chart. Unfavorable secondary factors can lower the natural position of the Curve from 1 to 20 percent. The Business Curve dropped five points through the fall of 1919.

The Business Curve shot upward 11 points above normal during January and February 1920, under the inflationary influence of Jupiter in conjunction with Neptune, semi-sextile Saturn and semi-sextile Pluto. This upturn was short-lived, however, for in March and April of 1920, the Business Curve dropped seven points due to the fact that Saturn had come within orb of the unfavorable 180 degree angle *(opposition aspect)* with Uranus. The Business Curve remained from four to five points above normal through August 1920, when the Curve turned sharply downward. This downturn of the Business Curve, which remained below the normal line for the next twenty months, was the beginning of the "Primary Post-War Depression."

The Primary Post-War Depression—1920-1922

Saturn was in opposition to the Midheaven of the New York Stock Exchange during the first three months of 1921 and Jupiter was in orb of a conjunction aspect with Saturn. Mars passing over the Midheaven of the same Chart was in unfavorable aspect to Saturn and Jupiter. This indicated falling stock prices, falling bond

Business Cycles and Stock Market Trends 1850-1950

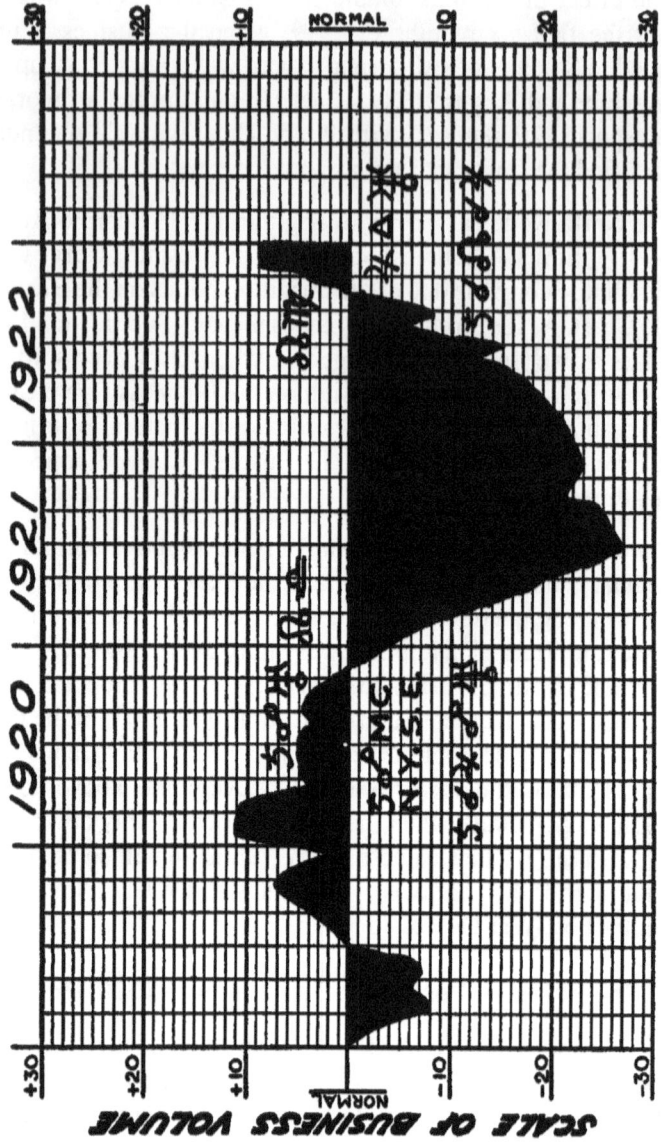

Primary Post-War Depression, 1920-1922

prices and high interest rates. The Business Curve dropped to 26 points below the normal line. During most of 1921 Saturn was in conjunction with Jupiter and both planets were in opposition aspect to Uranus. This double influence pointed to the depression experienced during 1921.

The Moon's North Node moved into Libra on February 28, 1921, and the technically correct position for the Business Curve was slightly above normal, where it would have been if it had not been for the presence of the unfavorable secondary factors mentioned above.

In October 1921, both Saturn and Jupiter moved into Libra and the Business Curve rose five points through December.

During 1922, a rapid recovery set in from the depression of the previous years and the Business Curve rose 22 points by September. During the first part of the year Saturn, Jupiter, and the North Node were in conjunction in Libra. During the last three months of 1922, Jupiter was in a favorable 120 degree angle with Uranus (*trine aspect*).

On September 16, 1922, the North Node moved into Virgo. This lifted the natural position of the Curve to a position slightly under the high point (*Leo*) on the Business Cycle Chart.

The combined influence of the North Node's passage into Virgo and the favorable Jupiter-Uranus aspect lifted the Business Curve 9 points above the normal line by the end of December 1922.

During the first four months of 1923, the Business Curve rose from 9 points above normal to 15 points above the normal line. This rise of 6 points was due to Jupiter being trine Uranus and semi-sextile Saturn.

From May through December 1923, the Business Curve dropped steadily, losing 11 points. This was due to the presence of the secondary factor, Uranus in opposition to the North Node. This unfavorable aspect lasted practically during the entire year.

In December 1923, Saturn formed an unfavorable sesquiquadrate aspect (135 *degrees*) with Uranus; it was in force through the fall of 1924.

Except for a three point rise in the Business Curve during January and February 1924, when Jupiter was in favorable aspect (*semi-sextile*, 30 *degrees*) to Saturn, the Business Curve dropped sharply below normal through November 1924. Uranus was in sesquiquadrate aspect to Saturn and in square aspect to Jupiter. The Curve reached its low of 13 points below normal in June.

The North Node moved into Leo, the sign on the "high" point of the Business Cycle Chart, April 4, 1924. This transit into Leo indicated that the technically correct position of the Business Curve had reached its high point and that business activity should be booming at this time if there were no unfavorable secondary factors present to keep the Business Curve down. Since there were present unfavorable secondary factors during 1924, as soon as they passed, the Business Curve was bound to rise and adjust itself to its technically correct position above the normal line. The Business Curve rose 13 points through the summer and fall and crossed the normal line in December. It had a further rise of 4 points by the end of the month, which marked the beginning of the three-year period of above normal prices known in history as the "Coolidge Prosperity Period."

Coolidge Prosperity Period—1925-1927

At the beginning of 1925, the Business Curve was standing at almost 9 points above normal. From January to October 1925, the Business Curve receded 5 points. Two secondary factors came into play during this period: (1) Saturn and Uranus formed a favorable trine aspect (120 *degrees)* during the spring and fall; (2) Uranus moved to the Midheaven of the New York Stock Exchange Chart.

The favorable aspect between Saturn and Uranus mitigated the influence of the elevated position of Uranus on the tenth house or

McWhirter Theory of Stock Market Forecasting

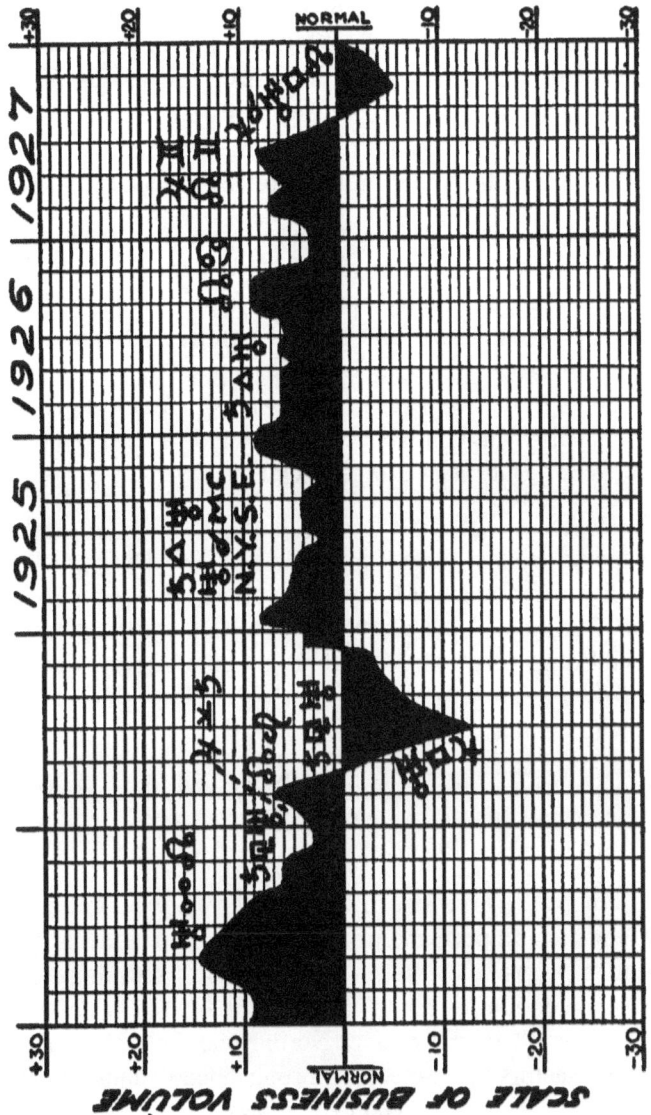

Coolidge Prosperity Period, 1925-1927

angle of the New York Stock Exchange Chart, which was originated by the writer and which gives an excellent key to the future trend of the Stock Market. Uranus stands for the unexpected, the unprecedented and the unusual. The fact that it was favorably aspected by Saturn pointed to the prosperity period at hand as well as the rise in the Stock Market. This period marked the beginning of the greatest Bull Market for stock prices in financial history.

As has been stated before in these pages, no planet has ever passed over the Midheaven of the New York Stock Exchange Chart which has not pointed out very definite changes in the trend of security prices, bonds, and general business activity. The passage of Uranus over this point was no exception to this rule. In fact, the wildest speculative wave in history took place during this transit. Uranus truly brought about the "unheard-of" and most precedent-breaking Bull Market in financial history.

The Business Curve rose 6 points during the fall of 1925, reaching 9 points above normal by January 1926. During 1926 the Curve fluctuated most of the year between 6 and 9 points above normal. During the latter part of October 1926, the Business Curve dropped from 9 points above normal to 4 points above normal due to the fact that Saturn moved out of orb of the favorable 120 degree angle with Uranus.

On October 25, 1925, the North Node had moved out of Leo into Cancer and this slight lowering of the technical position of the Business Curve (*see Business Cycle Chart*) was felt during 1926.

The Business Curve rose to 8 points above normal through June 1927, and then dropped sharply through the remainder of the year, reaching 5 points below normal in November. This drop was due to the conjunction aspect of Uranus and Jupiter in unfavorable square aspect (90 *degrees*) to the North Node. This combination of secondary factors was especially strong since Uranus and Jupiter were both on the Midheaven of the New York Stock Exchange Chart.

On May 13, 1927, the North Node moved into Gemini, the sign which strongly influences the United States. This transit indicated that the technical position of the Business Curve was now slightly above normal. The planet Jupiter in Gemini, however, together with the North Node, has an expansive influence on business in this country every 12 years when it goes through Gemini. *(The transit of Jupiter through the ruling sign of any country brings a period of prosperity and expansion if there is no decidedly opposing testimony.)* The passage of the North Node into Gemini in 1927 and the transit of Jupiter into Gemini in 1929 marked out the "Bull Market Boom" period in financial history, which will be long remembered in this country as one of the greatest prosperity periods of all times.

The Bull Market Boom, 1928-1929

During the first six months of 1928, the Business Curve stood between 2 and 3 points above normal due to the fact that Saturn was in unfavorable opposition aspect (180 *degrees)* to the North Node. The Business Curve rose 6 points in August as Jupiter, Uranus and the North Node were in favorable aspect. This combination of favorable secondary factors was also in force through the fall of 1928, along with a favorable 120 degree aspect *(trine)* between Saturn and Uranus. The Business Curve rose from 9 points above normal to 15 points above normal during the first six months of 1929. This was the high point reached by the Business Curve in the "Bull Market Boom." The high point for stock prices was reached on September 3, 1929. The average for Rails was 189 and the average for Industrials was 381.

On December 1, 1928, the North Node moved into Taurus. This was a warning signal six months in advance that the "Bull Market Boom" would soon be over. Taurus is the sign on the Business Cycle Chart which marks the transition point in the Business Cycle as the Business Curve goes from normal to low during a four-year period. The Business Curve, as well as the Stock Market, had to go lower in a short time, and traders could have been saved the terrific

Business Cycles and Stock Market Trends 1850-1950

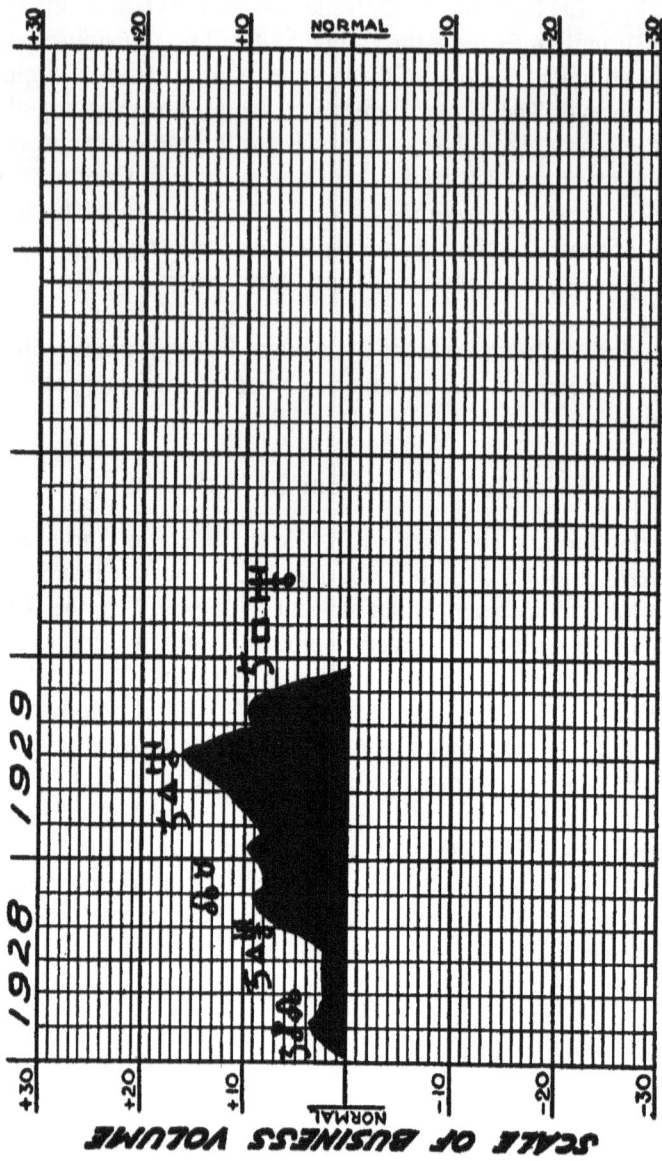

Bull Market Boom, 1928-1929

losses they suffered if this theory of forecasting the Market had been known.

The Wall Street Panic of 1929

This never-to-be-forgotten panic occurred October 24, 1929, culminating in the close of the New York Stock Exchange for adjustments on October 26, 1929.

The panic was clearly pointed out by the previous lunation (as all Stock Market crashes have been pointed out in the past).

The lunation, or New Moon, occurred October 2, 1929 in 8 degrees Libra, in exact opposition aspect (180 *degrees*) to the chaotic and epoch-making planet Uranus which was posited on the Midheaven of the New York Stock Exchange Chart. Uranus was the "key" planet to this crash since it had been occupying an elevated position for some time on this important angle of the New York Stock Exchange Chart. Uranus has the most unusual, revolutionary, unexpected, and epoch-making effects upon conditions, and surely this financial crash, *for which Uranus was responsible,* was epoch-making. It caught most traders unaware of danger, and then wiped them out. This panic, which saw Industrial Averages plummet from a high of 381 to a low of 198 by the middle of November, and Rail averages drop from a high of 189 to a low of 128 in the same length of time, marked the beginning of the severe "Secondary Post-War Depression" period, the effects of which have dominated the 1930s.

The Secondary Post-War Depression

From October through December 1929, the Business Curve dropped 16 points. Saturn moved into Capricorn November 30, and came within orb of an unfavorable square aspect (90 *degrees)* with Uranus. At the same time the North Node was in a favorable aspect with Uranus and this temporary favorable secondary factor lifted the Business Curve 2 points in January and February 1930. In March, however, the Business Curve turned downward under

Business Cycles and Stock Market Trends 1850-1950

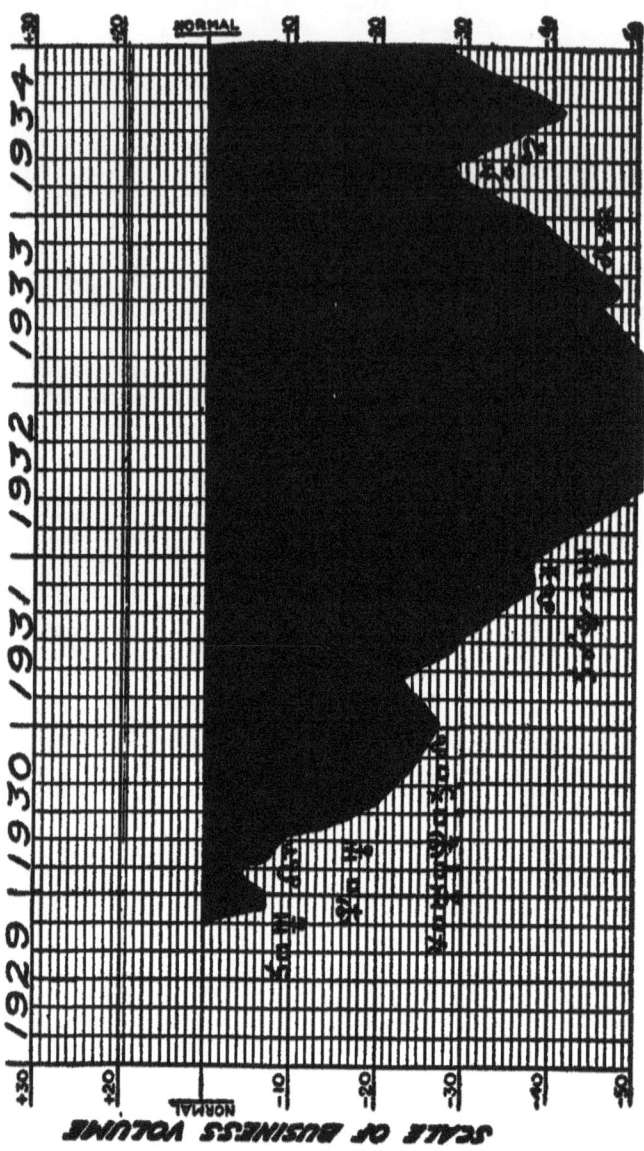

Secondary Post-War Depression, 1929-1934

the influence of the unfavorable Saturn-Uranus square aspect and by the end of 1930 the Business Curve was 27 points below the normal line.

On June 19, 1930, the North Node moved into Aries, indicating that the technical position of the Business Curve, without the presence of either favorable or unfavorable secondary factors, was now below normal and would be going still lower until the North Node moved into Aquarius, which is the low point on the Business Cycle Chart, July 28, 1933.

The powerful planet Pluto was going over the Ascendent of the New York Stock Exchange Chart during 1930 in unfavorable square aspect to Uranus on the Midheaven of this same chart. Jupiter was also in square aspect to Saturn, Uranus, Pluto, and the North Node.

During 1931, the Business Curve dropped 11 points lower than the preceding year and by the end of December was standing at 38 points below normal. Saturn was in unfavorable opposition (180 *degrees)* aspect to Pluto and Jupiter and in unfavorable square aspect to Uranus. Uranus was also in unfavorable square aspect to Pluto and Jupiter besides being in conjunction with the North Node. Such an array of powerful unfavorable secondary factors sent the Business Curve sharply downward during the year.

The election year, 1932, saw no let-up from the depression—unemployment, strikes, bank failures, poor business and hard times were felt over the entire country. The Democratic Party, which had been out of power since the Wilson Administration (*a period of* 12 *years*), was swept into power by an overwhelming and unprecedented victory. The Republican Party was in disgrace. Franklin Delano Roosevelt was the man of the hour. It is significant to mention here that Mr. Roosevelt is an Aquarian and when he took office the North Node had moved into Aquarius, the sign on the low point of the Business Cycle Chart, showing that business was at a low ebb and that Mr. Roosevelt was a man fitted by birth to handle the situation at that time. Even more significant is the fact that Mr. Hoover is a Leo type, the sign diametrically opposed to Aquarius, since it is its polar opposite. Leo is on the high point of the Business Cycle Chart, which indicates that Mr. Hoover was not fitted by birth to handle the depression as Mr. Roosevelt was. Mr. Hoover, as it would be expected, favored the Capitalists and moneyed interests. Mr. Roosevelt, on the other hand, has championed the cause of the little man. The two men stand for totally different things and it is doubtful if either one can ever see the other's governmental viewpoint.

In fairness to both great men it is not amiss to digress long enough here to state that Mr. Hoover was not responsible for the depression and Mr. Roosevelt was not responsible for the recovery. Both processes came about as a natural order of things—the ebb and flow of cyclic change in finance. Mr. Hoover's views were not fitted, however, to work in harmony with the process of recovery and Mr. Roosevelt's views were. That made all the difference.

The Business Curve dropped from 38 points below normal to 51 points below normal by the end of 1932. The entire country was in the midst of the worst depression ever experienced and business of all forms was at a standstill.

The North Node had moved into Pisces January 7, 1932, lowering the Business Curve's technical position further below the normal line. The secondary factor, however, which caused such a severe drop in the Business Curve and Stock Market averages, was the unfavorable square aspect (90 *degrees*) between Uranus on the Midheaven of the New York Stock Exchange Chart and Pluto on the Ascendant of this same Chart. Due to the slow movement of these planets, this aspect was in force during all of 1931, 1932, and 1933.

On July 28, 1933, the North Node moved into Aquarius, the sign on the low point of the Business Cycle Chart. This transit indicated, according to this theory, that (1) the Business Curve would go no lower and that (2) with the passage of the North Node out of Aquarius, the trend of the Business Curve would slowly swing upward for four years. During 1933, the Business Curve rose 10 points, but it was still 40 percent below normal at the end of the year. During the first part of 1934, Saturn came into conjunction with the North Node and this unfavorable secondary factor depressed the Business Curve about five points. Business did not show much progress during 1934.

The real recovery, according to this theory of forecasting economic cycles, began when the North Node passed out of the sign Aquarius and into the sign of Capricorn February 13, 1935. Business was still far below normal, but it moved sharply upward toward the normal line during 1935. During the last week of March 1935, a very favorable secondary factor came into force and this aspect sent the Business Curve upward much faster than it ordinarily would have gone. This secondary factor, which acted as an accelerator on the Business Curve, was the sextile (60 *degrees*) aspect between Saturn in Pisces and Uranus in Taurus.

This was the beginning of an upswing in the Stock Market, which lasted for approximately thirteen months and which was accompanied by marked trade improvement. The year 1935 was hailed in Wall Street as the most encouraging period since 1929. The Associated Press average of 60 stocks stood at 55 at the end of the year after rising from the year's low of 34.8 on March 18, 1935. Recurring political and financial crises during the year did not deter the upturn of the Stock Market. Sixteen public utility companies advanced around 140 percent from their lows to the end of the year. The reason Utilities were so prominent in their rise, especially during the latter half of June and July, the latter part of October and the first half of November 1935, was due to the fact that most of them are incorporated under the earth (*Taurus, Virgo, Capricorn*) and water signs (*Pisces, Cancer, and Scorpio*). Steels likewise come under the rulership of the earth and water signs and they too had a strong rise during this year.

The presence of Saturn in Pisces (*water sign*) in favorable aspect to Uranus in Taurus (*earth sign*) and in favorable aspect to Jupiter in Scorpio (*water sign*) brought about the upturn in share values of these two prominent Groups during 1935.

The year 1936 opened bullish for the Stock Market and business continued to improve. The rise in the Stock Market during 1936 was one of the best in history. Except for a break in April 1936, and minor recessions during August and November 1936, the Bull Market in Stocks which began in March 1935, continued steadily upward in 1936. This was a new all-time record for longevity. The average rise in stock market values was 25 percent in 1936.

The break in stock market prices, which came in April 1936, was clearly indicated by this theory. The rise in share values culminated April 6, 1936, as Venus passed over the Midheaven of the New York Stock Exchange and no favorable planets followed this transit over this important point. Furthermore, the favorable aspect between Saturn and Uranus was no longer in force and these two planets were forming an unfavorable semi-square aspect (45 *degrees*) with each other. Without the presence of the favorable secondary factor, share values as well as the Business Curve were Bound to have a technical reaction to adjust themselves to their rightful position, since the favorable aspect between Saturn and Uranus had sent the Business Curve upward much higher than it ordinarily would have been.

The slump in stock market prices, which occurred April 27, 1936, was pointed out at the lunation of April 21, 1936. At that time the New Moon was sesquiquadrate Neptune, conjunction Uranus, semi-square Saturn, and trine Jupiter. The aspect which pointed to the drop in stocks was the unfavorable aspect (135 *degrees*) with Neptune. Every break in the Stock Market, when there have been no planets transiting the Midheaven of the New York Stock Exchange Chart, has been pointed out at the preceding lunation by a conjunction or an unfavorable aspect to Neptune or Mars, the two planetary rulers of the Midheaven of the New York Stock

Exchange Chart. Pisces and Aries, the two signs which are placed on the tenth angle or Midheaven of this Chart, are ruled by Neptune and Mars respectively. If there is a planet passing through or transiting over this angle of the Chart, it must be considered along with Neptune and Mars, at any lunation, when determining the future monthly trend for the stock market's action.

When a reaction in the stock market is indicated for any month, it is always well to notice the days following the lunation when the Moon passes through the signs which are placed on the angles of the chart of the New York Stock Exchange. These signs are Cancer, Libra, Capricorn, and Aries. The signs Virgo and Pisces are also co-rulers of the fourth and tenth angles and the days when the Moon passes through these should also be watched. It usually will be found that the break will occur on one of these days. This is what happened in April 1936. On April 27, 1936, when the break occurred, the Moon was in Cancer, the sign which is the Ascendant of the New York Stock Exchange Chart.

The slight recessions of August and November 1936 were partly seasonal dullness and occurred when the Sun was passing through the mutable signs of Virgo and Sagittarius. These signs being in square and opposition aspect to the Midheaven of the New York Stock Exchange Chart often point out the months they rule as dull months both for business and the stock market generally. *(Gemini is the other mutable sign of the Mutable Square, but it is the sign which strongly influences the United States; therefore, the Sun's passage through this sign does not generally bring a reaction or dull period in the stock market and business each year.)*

The year 1936 marks the fourth consecutive year that share values had shown an uptrend in price. The Dow-Jones Industrial Average at the end of 1933 stood at 99.90; at the end of 1934 at 104.04; at the end of 1935 at 144.13; and at the end of 1936 at 179.90.

The movement of the Groups during the year shows that Industrials had the most consistent strength during 1936. Utilities moved in a narrow price range the last half of the year. Rails showed the widest gains and losses as a whole. Commodities experienced a Bull Market during 1936. The Bond Market also turned sharply upward in price value, advancing 7 percent. Second grade Rail bonds had a spectacular rise of 23 percent in the Dow-Jones Averages. Recovery from the depression of the early 1930s was the feature financial and business fact of the formative year of 1936.

1937, which was forecast ahead of time as another year of greater prosperity, turned out to be not so bullish after all. Forecasts for 1937, except the published ones by the writer based on the theory in this book, all saw greater profits in the Stock Market for the year ahead.

The published articles of the writer, while stating that the Business Curve was upward during 1937, warned that Saturn was approaching 24 degrees Pisces and that a recession in stock and bond shares would be likely to occur. The Midheaven of the New York Stock Exchange Chart is governed by 24 to 28 degrees Pisces and Saturn's passage over this crucial point would certainly leave its mark, inasmuch as no major planet has ever passed over the Midheaven of the New York Stock Exchange Chart without indicating very definite changes in the stock market and subsequently business.

The North Node had passed into Sagittarius September 1, 1936, and this transit placed the technical position of the Business Curve slightly below normal. However, Saturn's movement to this elevated position on the Exchange Chart, forecast the drop in security prices for the year as well as the slump in bonds.

The lunation occurred March 12, 1937, in 21 degrees Pisces, in conjunction with Saturn (*which was in* 24 *degrees Pisces on the exact angle of the Midheaven of the New York Stock Exchange Chart*), in opposition aspect to Neptune (*one of the rulers of the Midheaven of the New York Stock Exchange Chart*), in semi-square aspect to Uranus, sextile aspect to Jupiter, and semi-square aspect to Venus. On the same day that the lunation occurred, Federal Bonds slumped after being easy all week. (*Saturn had been in 24 degrees Pisces since the sixth of March,* 1937!) When the lunation fell in conjunction with Saturn, it set off the Bond slump and gave a warning that a drop in stocks was bound to follow soon, since Saturn's elevated position on this Chart affected stock prices also. It is interesting to note here that Government Bonds were at a high the last week in January 1937, when Venus was in 24 degrees Pisces, in exact conjunction with the Midheaven of this same Chart. This slump in bonds was registered as the greatest turnover in Government Bonds since December 1920, and at that time Saturn was in 24 degrees Virgo, in exact opposition to the Midheaven of the New York Stock Exchange Chart.

The first symptoms of the coming Stock Market decline occurred on April 7, 1937. Leading issues were off 1 to 6 points upon the rumor of a Gold price cut. Commodities cracked with weakness, engulfing almost every commodity from metals to grains. London and Amsterdam Markets were equally affected. The lunation of March 12, 1937 had forecast this drop through the opposition aspect to Neptune at the lunation. On April 7, the Sun, Moon, and Mercury were in unfavorable aspect to Neptune.

On April 26, 1937, there was a slump on the London Exchange which caused a drop in Wall Street. (*England comes under the rulership of the sign of Aries; therefore, Saturn's passage into Aries marked out lower bond and stock market values for that country.*)

On April 28, 1937, stocks slumped again on the New York Stock Exchange, reaching new 1937 lows and losing 25 percent of their value acquired since March 1935. This drop was pointed out at the lunation of April 11, 1937. The New Moon at this time was in unfavorable sesquiquadrate aspect to Neptune, in semi-sextile aspect to Saturn, in square aspect to Jupiter, in unfavorable sesquiquadrate aspect to Mars, and in conjunction aspect with Venus. The two unfavorable aspects to both rulers (*Neptune and*

Mars) of the Midheaven of the Chart of the New York Stock Exchange dearly indicated this drop. There was a rally in stocks after this break which carried stocks to 190 in the Dow-Jones Industrial Averages by the first part of August. This rally brought stocks to within five points of the recovery high of March 1937. At the lunation of August 6, 1937, the New Moon was in semi-sextile aspect to Neptune, in unfavorable square aspect to Uranus, and in unfavorable sesquiquadrate aspect to Saturn, which is now a "key" planet in analyzing the trend of stock market prices due to its elevated position on the Midheaven of the Chart of the New York Stock Exchange. The lunation was also in unfavorable semi-square aspect to Venus and in favorable semi-sextile aspect to Mercury, both of which are minor aspects in effect. The unfavorable aspect to Saturn at the lunation indicated the downturn in stock prices. On August 14, 1937, the Sun formed an unfavorable 135 degree angle *(sesquiquadrate aspect)* with Saturn, and the stock market averages turned downward. Saturn is the planet representative of fear. Its elevated position on the tenth angle *(Midheaven) of* the New York Stock Exchange Chart indicated that fear would be a dominant mental factor influencing market trading. Furthermore, the tenth angle of this same Chart represents the credit, reputation, and heads of the New York Stock Exchange, and Saturn's position here represented trouble in this division of the New York Stock Exchange Chart. This Chart, which is the original work of the writer, has clearly mirrored the 1937-38 history of the Stock Market.

The lunation of September 4, 1937 fell in conjunction with Neptune and in unfavorable square aspect to Mars, the two planetary rulers of the New York Stock Exchange Chart's tenth angle or Midheaven. This configuration clearly pointed out a drop in the Stock Market during September 1937. On September 7, 1937, as the Moon *(symbolic of the public mind)* moved through Libra in opposition aspect to Saturn *(fear)*, a wave of selling took place on the London Exchange with the selling of "Americans," which had a drastic reaction on Wall Street, causing numerous issues to drop from 1 to 10 points in a very active market. This was the worst drop since September 24, 1931. There was a share turnover of 1,700,000 shares. As the Sun moved into conjunction with Neptune and in unfavorable square aspect (90 *degrees*) with Mars, the two rulers of the Midheaven of the New York Stock Exchange Chart, stocks dropped from $1.00 to $6.00 a share after the break on Tuesday, September 7, 1937. This was the greatest decline since October 17, 1930. Several individual issues were down as much as 13 points. The Industrial average was off 8.38 points.

On September 24, 1937, as the Sun moved in opposition to Saturn, which is placed in a key position on the Exchange Chart's Midheaven, heavy fear selling, both here and abroad, took place. As many as 538 issues plummeted to new lows, with stock prices losing two billion in value.

The crashes in the Stock Market, which took place on October 18 and 19, 1937, were pointed out by the lunation or New Moon of October 4, 1937. At this time the Moon was in opposition to Saturn and in square aspect to Mars. Mars and Saturn were in unfavorable square aspect to each other. On the 18th of October, the Moon was in conjunction with Saturn and in unfavorable square aspect to Mars. This break was the worst for stocks since 1930. On the 19th of October 1937, stocks slumped again with the heaviest selling in four years. There were 932 lows with 7,287,990 shares traded. This was the greatest volume since July 21, 1933. Venus was in opposition to Saturn on this day.

Saturn rules fear and this present recession has been the result of public fear. The mind of the trading public has been stimulated to believe in such unreal states of consciousness as lack, loss, depression, and bad business. These conditions could not manifest themselves in actuality, if they were not thought and believed first. In the near future, economists and Governmental heads will control booms and depressions through the realization that booms and depressions are man-made and the outward results of men's thoughts. The Government will then be the master of economic conditions in this country instead of its helpless victim in times of depression.

At the end of 1937, Bond prices were 11.9 percent lower than at the end of 1936. The Dow-Jones Average for Industrials was 32.8 percent lower than it was at the end of 1936. Dow-Jones Rail Averages were 45.1 percent below what they were a year ago. The Dow-Jones Utilities Average was 41.6 percent below what it was at the end of 1936. Business, in general, was 23.5 percent lower than at the end of 1936. Commodity prices also were lower than a year ago. The year 1937 which had begun so bullish ended definitely bearish.

The "Recession of 1937" continued into part of 1938, with only brief rallies in the Stock Market. The first half of the year brought about the failure of Richard Whitney and Co. and the subsequent reorganization of the New York Stock Exchange. Mr. Whitney was five times President of the New York Stock Exchange, and one of the most prominent members of the Exchange. His conviction for embezzlement reflected on the credit *(tenth house matter on the Exchange Chart)* of the New York Stock Exchange. Saturn's position elevated in the Midheaven (*tenth house*) of the New York Stock Exchange pointed out trouble in regard to officials and the credit standing of the New York Stock Exchange. This brought about a change in government of the Exchange with the installation of the first paid president of the New York Stock Exchange in history.

The month of March 1938 saw Stock Market prices drift lower with business activity dull. The lunation of March 2, 1938 fell in unfavorable opposition aspect to Neptune, one of the rulers of the Midheaven of the New York Stock Exchange and a planet which is usually unfavorably aspected at any lunation preceding a drop in the Stock Market. One of the worst drops of the month came on March 29, 1938, when a selling wave took place and stocks plunged to 1932 levels. Stocks went to three-year lows with the entire list off. The Dow-Jones Industrial Average dropped 5.33

points. As many as 1,720,000 shares changed hands. The Moon in Pisces on this date was in opposition aspect to Neptune, and as it passed over the degree and place of the lunation, the unfavorable aspects of the New Moon of March 2, 1938 came into effect.

On March 23, 1938, the North Node moved into Scorpio, the sign which is placed on the "normal or transition" point of the Business Cycle Chart. This indicated that the Business Curve should adjust itself to normal if no unfavorable planetary aspects were present to act as secondary factors, which would keep the Business Curve below normal.

A favorable secondary factor of minor strength came into play in April and this aspect will be in effect most of 1938. It is the semi-sextile aspect between Saturn and Uranus. Stock did improve in value and business activity assumed renewed vigor during the summer months of 1938 and on through the rest of the year. Saturn in its "key" position on the Midheaven of the New York Stock Exchange is still unfavorable, but the fact that it is favorably aspected by Uranus will mitigate this unfavorable influence to a great extent. The Business Curve, having reached its technical "normal" point according to this theory, also indicated that Business would improve and stocks advance during 1938. This was a good year to buy. The semi-sextile aspect is not as strong as the favorable sextile aspect (60 *degree angle)* between Saturn and Uranus which took share values upward so strongly during 1935-1936. It just has half the strength of that aspect, but it is aided by the fact that the North Node is in Scorpio and has reached the technically "normal" point on the Business Cycle Chart. This fact should help the Business Curve with the presence of the minor favorable secondary factor, go slightly above normal during the last six months of the year. During 1935-36, the technically correct position of the Business Curve was "below normal," but the favorable secondary factor of 60 degrees between Saturn and Uranus was very strong and this lifted the Curve sharply. The first half of 1938 did not look as strong as the last half of the year since the Saturn-Uranus aspect did not come within orb until April 1938, and was not exact until June.

Despite the fact that the Saturn-Uranus aspect was in force during the latter half of 1938, the lunations from August to the end of the year unfavorably aspect Neptune; therefore, it is not possible to state which condition will outweigh the other and trading caution is advised towards the end of the year. Two forces seem to be pulling against each other during this year.

1939

During 1939, two astronomical factors come into play which will affect the trend of stock prices, bond prices, and general business activity. The first factor is the passage of Jupiter into the sign of Pisces where it will pass over the Midheaven of the New York Stock Exchange Chart. Jupiter's position here indicates rising stock market prices, rising bond prices and the return of the prestige of the New York Stock Exchange. The summer months do not appear as strong as the spring and fall. No planet has ever passed over the Midheaven of the New York Stock Exchange Chart which has not brought definite changes in the security and bond markets. Business has usually followed the Stock Market's trend.

Jupiter, unlike Saturn, is a planet of expansion, and favors prosperity and the upturn of security prices and business generally. Even though Jupiter has Saturn in the Midheaven with it also, Saturn will have moved far enough away not to cause much trouble. Therefore, 1939 will prosper the new organization of the New York Stock Exchange and the trading public will renew its confidence once more in the market.

The second astronomical factor which will play an important part in business activity during 1939 is the fact that the North Node passes out of Scorpio on October 10, 1939, and into the sign of Libra. This indicates that the Business Curve is now going from normal to high on the Business Cycle Chart and, if there are no unfavorable secondary factors present to lower the Curve, Business activity should go slightly above normal during the next twelve months.

From the joint testimony of the astronomical factors involved, it is evident that 1939 should be a very good year both for business and the stock market, making allowances, of course, from time to time, for any temporary dullness that is apt to occur as part of daily and monthly trends.

What of the Future—1940-1950?

The next ten years will mark one of the most crucial decades in the history of this country.

The North Node will be going through the signs Libra, Virgo, and Leo during a four year period, 1940-44. This indicates that the technical position of the Business Curve will be going from normal to high and that the Business Curve will reach its "high" point as the North Node transits Leo during 1943 and 1944. Business activity should be above normal during this four-year period, if there are no unfavorable secondary planetary factors present to lower the Curve. This is the basic underlying framework upon which the secondary factors will work. On the Business Cycle Chart these signs are going from normal to above normal, with the sign Leo marking the "high" point.

From June 1944 to July 1947, the North Node will be passing through Cancer and Gemini and will reach the sign of Taurus in July 1947. During this three year period, the Business Curve will be slowly going from "high" to "normal" on the Business Cycle Chart or business activity will be slowly going from "above normal" activity to "normal."

When the North Node reaches Taurus in July 1947, this is a warning signal that the Business Curve has reached its technically normal position and that this transit marks out a transition period before the Business Curve turns definitely downward for a four-year period.

Saturn and Uranus will also be in orb of a conjunction aspect during 1940, 1941, and 1942 in Taurus. Saturn and Uranus in con-

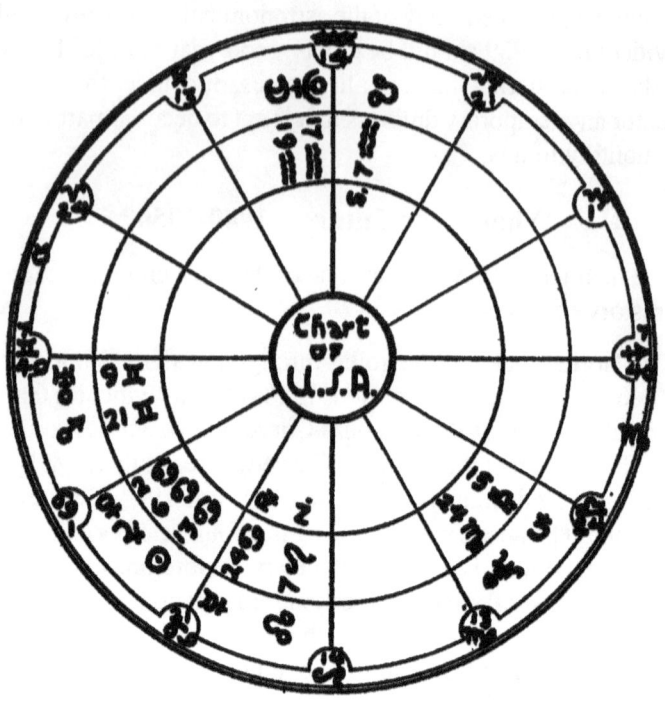

Chart of the United States of America

junction aspect usually brings declining prices, depression, and financial panics. This is a warning ahead of time to the governmental heads of this country that this country is headed for a more severe depression than the one which we have just been through unless steps are taken now to prevent its occurrence.

From May 1941 until June 1942, Jupiter will be in the sign of Gemini, which strongly influences the United States. This will mitigate to some extent the unfavorable influence of the Saturn and Uranus conjunction. Jupiter's passage through Gemini is usually accompanied by rising prices and bullish business conditions. Two sets of financial conditions will mark this period due to the presence of both favorable and unfavorable secondary factors.

The presence of three major planets, Saturn, Jupiter, and Uranus, in orb of a conjunction aspect with each other in the sign of Taurus portend drastic and unusual conditions affecting this country during the last half of 1940 and the first half of 1941. Now is the time to prepare for the future and prevent the happening of conditions which we do not want to occur.

In May 1942, both Saturn and Uranus enter the sign of Gemini, which depicts conditions affecting the United States as a whole. This conjunction of these two powerful planets in the sign ruling the United States is very significant. Depression and financial difficulties will engross the entire country unless the most drastic steps are taken by those at the head of our Government. This configuration of planets is even more significant when the fact is taken into consideration that the transit of Uranus through Gemini every 84 years has brought war to this country. In 1776, Uranus was in Gemini and we had the Revolutionary War. Then, 84 years later (it takes Uranus 84 years to pass through the twelve signs of the zodiac and return to its starting point), Uranus was again in Gemini, and the War between the States occurred in 1860. Since the Civil War, Uranus has not been in the sign of Gemini, but goes into that sign in May 1942. It is doubly significant at this time since it is in conjunction with Saturn, also in Gemini, and will be placed in this relationship through June 1944. Uranus has never passed through Gemini without bringing war, depression, and declining prices. Saturn has never passed through Gemini during the past 72 years without bringing a business depression, financial panic or war. Since 1830, Saturn has passed through the sign of Gemini three times and each transit has marked a critical period in the history of this country. Saturn was in Gemini in 1855-56. The Panic of 1857 followed this transit. The years 1883-84-85 again saw Saturn in the sign of Gemini and the Panic and Depression of 1884 took place. Saturn was again in Gemini from 1912 to 1914. This transit brought about the entrance of this country into the World War and the subsequent closing of the New York Stock Exchange.

In view of this imposing testimony, taken when Saturn and Uranus have passed through Gemini singly, it is little wonder that the combined strength of these two planets portend a most critical time in this country's history. This combination of planetary influence points out war, depression, governmental change, social upheaval, and a financial panic. None of this unpleasant picture has to materialize if steps are made now to acquaint our Governmental heads with the laws that govern our universe.

A knowledge of astrology is the only way out. It is doubtful, though, that mankind will do anything about it, for they are unwilling to learn how the majority of our people have reacted to planetary stimuli in the past.

During 1944, 1945, and 1946, Saturn will pass through the sign of Cancer, which rules the Ascendant of the New York Stock Exchange Chart, and a sign which strongly influences the United States also. This indicates some drastic changes in the financial world, the New York Stock Exchange itself, and in the Government during these three years.

Uranus will be in Gemini until June 1949. Thus it will be in this country's ruling sign for about seven years.

During October, November, and December 1944, and during the first nine months of 1945, Saturn and Uranus will be in a minor favorable semi-sextile aspect (30 *degrees*). This may result in improved business conditions and an upturn in security prices during this time. This aspect, however, is of minor strength and it is hard to tell just how much of a rise, if any, it will bring.

During the fall of 1947, during all of 1948, and until the fall of 1949, a very favorable secondary factor will be in force which should cause stocks to rise, bonds to rise, and business to boom generally. This aspect is the major favorable sextile aspect (60 *degree angle*) between Saturn and Uranus. It was this aspect which caused the rise in security prices during 1935-37.

The Moon's North Node moves into Aries January 31, 1949. This indicates that the technical position of the Business Curve is now below normal, even though favorable secondary factors keep the Curve above normal until the aspect passes. This occurs in the late fall of 1949.

During 1950, Saturn is in the sign of Virgo and is moving toward an opposition aspect with the Midheaven of the New York Stock Exchange Chart. This indicates that in the fall of 1950 bond and security prices will go lower and possibly slump.

On August 19, 1950, the Moon's North Node passes into Pisces, taking the technical normal position of the Business Curve further below the normal line. In December 1950, Saturn forms a very unfavorable square (90 *degrees*) aspect with Uranus, and prices will go much lower with business activity far below normal. Stocks and bonds will be in a Bear Market in the midst of a depression period well into 1951.

The information given in this ten-year general outlook will make money for those individuals who plan their financial future ahead of time. For those who are not interested in a planned financial future, there is little chance that they will be able to survive the next decade with its financial upheavals. The old hit-and-miss system, guess-work, and methods which have worked during the preceding business cycles will be of little use in the complicated ten years we are to go through shortly.

Time will confirm the truth contained in this forecast. The recognition of this method of forecasting economic cycles should be brought to the attention of the present Administration, and particularly to the attention of those who hope to be in power after 1940. Much can be done by the present Administration in the remaining two years (this is being written in early 1938) to prevent the collapse of our economic structure in the future, but the laws of nature governing supply and demand must be recognized and utilized now.

Business Cycles and Stock Market Trends 1850-1950

Chapter III

How to Forecast Monthly and Daily Trends on the New York Stock Exchange

The most reliable method for forecasting monthly trends on the New York Stock Exchange for any desired month in advance is to take the planetary positions at the lunation of the previous month and place these planetary positions in their right positions on the chart of the New York Stock Exchange. A copy of this chart, which was originated by the writer after a long period of economic research, accompanies this chapter.

The best way to learn how to forecast Stock Market trends in advance is to take an example month and work it out. After doing a number of charts for months in advance and then watching the reaction of the Stock Market as it actually takes place, anyone can soon learn to get a quick off-hand knowledge of what to expect. The value of this method lies in the fact that it tells you at any time in advance what month the Stock Market is apt to have a sharp drop or what month it is apt to be strongly bullish. No other method used today by chart-readers offers such advantages.

For an "example month," when a lower trend for stocks was dearly pointed out, let us take the month of March 1938. The entire

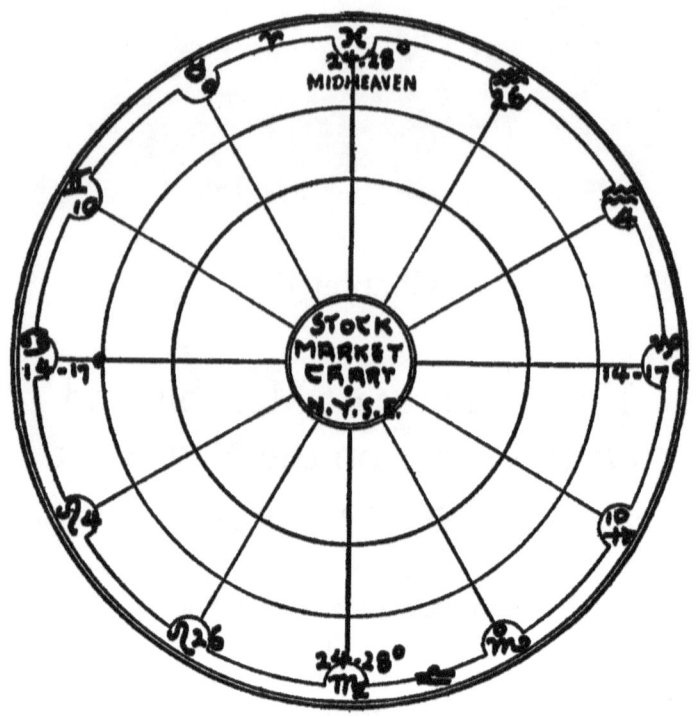

New York Stock Exchange Stock Market Chart

month was marked by a drop in the various stock market averages and many stocks dropped to 1932 lows. How was this fact pointed out?

Each New Moon or lunation occurs every twenty-eight days and that this lunation, by the angular relationship of the planets at the time of the New Moon, points out the trend of the New York Stock Market during the coming twenty-eight days.

The nearest lunation, or New Moon, which precedes the month of March occurred March 2, 1938. (As a rule the lunation affecting the coming month is given in the month before, which in this case would be February 1938. The Ephemeris, however, states that there was "no New Moon in February"; so the lunation of March 2, 1938 is used to give the indications for the month of March.)

On March 2, 1938, at the time of the lunation, the positions of the planets were as follows: Sun 10 degrees Pisces; Moon 10 degrees Pisces; Neptune 20 degrees Virgo retrograde; Uranus 10 degrees Taurus; Saturn 4 degrees Aries; Jupiter 16 degrees Aquarius; Mars 22 degrees Aries; Venus 17 degrees Pisces; Mercury 5 degrees Pisces. The Moon's North Node, which defines the general curve of economic cycles, was in 1 degree Sagittarius. These planets placed around a skeleton New York Stock Exchange Chart pointed out, by their positions and angular relationships to each other, the unstable Stock Market condition of March 1938.

It is necessary in this subject as well as in any other subject to use abbreviations and symbols whenever possible to conserve both time and energy. It is easy to place the signs with their degrees around the skeleton chart of the New York Stock Exchange whereas it is awkward and tedious to write the words and degrees, out on the chart. From now on the abbreviations and "short-hand" symbols for the signs and planets as well as their angles will be used in this chapter and other parts of the book. therefore a brief table is given here for readers to familiarize themselves with these symbols, and the more quickly these symbols are learned, the easier it will be to give a quick and accurate judgment of stock conditions at any time.

The Twelve Signs

1. Aries	♈	7. Libra	♎
2. Taurus	♉	8. Scorpio	♏
3. Gemini	♊	9. Sagittarius	♐
4. Cancer	♋	10. Capricorn	♑
5. Leo	♌	11. Aquarius	♒
6. Virgo	♍	12. Pisces	♓

The Ten Known Planets

1. Mars	♂	Aries	♈
2. Venus	♀	Taurus, Libra	♉, ♎
3. Mercury	☿	Gemini, Virgo	♊, ♍
4. Moon	☽	Cancer	♋
5. Sun	☉	Leo	♌
6. Pluto	♀	Scorpio	♏
7. Jupiter	♃	Sagittarius	♐
8. Saturn	♄	Capricorn	♑
9. Uranus	♅	Aquarius	♒
10. Neptune	♆	Pisces	♓

The Sun and Moon are not strictly planets in an astronomical sense, but in this work they are so labeled to simplify matters.

It also will be noticed that two planets have rulership over two signs each. This is due to the fact that there are only ten planets known. Like the chemist, we use what we have, although we know at some time two planets will be discovered which rule Taurus and Gemini. However, every planet has a sign in which it is almost as strong as in the sign it rules; therefore, it is alright to use Venus and Mercury as the rulers of Taurus and Gemini until research in astronomy gives us the two missing planets.

It is also necessary to know a few elementary facts regarding the chart of the New York Stock Exchange. These facts apply to all charts, and they should be learned carefully.

Each chart has twelve sections, one for each sign of the zodiac. The signs placed on these twelve cusps or spokes are arranged counter-clockwise, and so are the planets. Each sign has 30 degrees in it and the degree which falls on the cusp tells where a planet is to be placed on the chart. For instance, on the example chart for March, the Sun (☉) and Moon (☽) fell in 10 degrees Pisces. Since this degree falls before 24-28 degrees Pisces (♓), which is the sign on the tenth cusp, the Sun and Moon fall in the ninth section of the chart instead of the tenth section or "house." The planet Uranus, on this chart, fell in 10 degrees Taurus (♉) and since zero degrees Taurus falls on the eleventh section of the chart, Uranus actually falls in the eleventh section or "house." (The twelve sections of a chart are called "houses.")

It sometimes happens that a sign will be intercepted in a "house," making two signs with their corresponding planetary rulers, governors of that particular section. This is due to the fact that charts set up for different latitudes "cut" the zodiac into different sized sections.

Most charts will have degrees and minutes on the cusp of the first house or Ascendant, but it will be noticed that the Chart of the New York Stock Exchange has the connotation "14-17 degrees Cancer (♋)" on the first house or Ascendant and the notation 24-28 degrees Pisces (♓) on the tenth house or Midheaven of the same Chart. Do not let this confuse you. It merely means that these degrees have been found to include a sensitive area in connection with stock market trends whenever subject to planetary transits.

Most of the terms and words used in this work, not generally used in the average person's vocabulary, are included in the "*Glossary*," where they can be found for ready reference at any time. An explanation here, however, was deemed advisable inasmuch as few persons can understand a chart who have not had some instruction along the above lines.

The chart of the New York Stock Exchange becomes more comprehensible with the above facts in mind.

Any month up to 1950 may be forecast for any time in advance by placing the lunation Planetary positions affecting the month in question around a copy of the New York Stock Exchange Chart.

After the planets have been placed around the chart in their proper house positions, the following facts must be sought:

Monthly and Daily Trends on the New York Stock Exchange

(1) If there are any major planets placed in the tenth house or Midheaven of the chart; if there are any planets placed in the first house or Ascendant of the chart; and if there are any planets in the fourth house or seventh house of the chart. The angles listed here are given in the order of their importance; that is, tenth, first, fourth and seventh, in diagnosing market conditions.

If there are major planets (that is, all the planets except Venus and Mercury) in the houses or sections mentioned they become so-called "key" planets, for aspects to them at a lunation become highly important in making market forecasts.

Planets on the Midheaven or tenth house are the most important in making judgment of stock trends for the coming month. These planets are to be taken into account along with the two rulers of the tenth house or Midheaven of the New York Stock Exchange Chart. These rulers are Neptune and Mars because they rule Pisces and Aries respectively, which are placed on this section of the chart.

(2) If the lunation or New Moon is in favorable or unfavorable aspect to Neptune or Mars, the two rulers of the Midheaven of the New York Stock Exchange Chart; if the lunation or New Moon is in favorable aspect to the "key" planet or in unfavorable aspect to the "key" planet (if there is one).

(3) The last point, which should be noted particularly, in connection with market conditions is the fact whether Saturn and Uranus are in favorable aspect to each other; in unfavorable aspect to each other; or not in aspect at all.

If Saturn and Uranus are in favorable aspect with each other that is, placed 120, 60, or 30 degrees from each other, the Stock Market will rise for the extent of this aspect. The aspects are given in the order of their strength or importance. That is, the trine aspect, sextile aspect and semi-sextile aspect.

If Saturn and Uranus are in unfavorable aspect with each other, that is, placed in conjunction, 180, 90, 135 or 45 degrees from each other, the trend of stocks will be down for the extent of the aspect.

The conjunction aspect between Saturn and Uranus, if powerfully aspected by Jupiter or Neptune, from a favorable angle, is variable and may or may not point out a drop in the Stock Market. The unfavorable aspects between Saturn and Uranus are listed in the order of their strength or importance, that is, the conjunction, opposition, square, sesquiquadrate and semi-square aspect. There are 360 degrees in a chart and it is an easy matter to determine whether planets are in favorable or unfavorable aspect to each other by simple arithmetic. However, for readers who are not mathematically inclined, the following table will give the information whether Saturn and Uranus are in favorable or unfavorable aspect at any time. This information can be used to determine the relationship between any other of the planets as well.

* * *

Planets which are in the same sign of the zodiac, and within 9 degrees of each other, are in conjunction aspect. The symbol for the conjunction aspect is ☌. (For example, a planet in 2 degrees Aries and a planet in 7 degrees aspect are in conjunction aspect, because they are within 9 degrees of each other. A planet in 1 degree Aries and a planet in 10 degrees Aries are in conjunction aspect because they are within 9 degrees of each other, etc.).

Planets which are placed one sign apart, or 30 degrees apart, are in semi-sextile aspect. Allow an orb of 3 degrees either way. The symbol for the semi-sextile aspect is ⚺.

Planets which are two signs apart are in sextile aspect (60 degrees) if they are within 5 degrees of each other. The symbol for the sextile aspect is ✶.

Planets which are one and a half signs apart are in semi-square aspect (45 degrees) if they are within 3 degrees of each other. The symbol for the semi-square aspect is ∠.

Planets which are placed three signs apart are in square aspect (90 degrees) if they are within 5 degrees of each other. The symbol for the square aspect is □.

Monthly and Daily Trends on the New York Stock Exchange

Planets which are four signs apart are in trine aspect (120 degrees) if they are within 5 degrees of each other. The symbol for the trine aspect is △.

Planets which are four and a half signs apart are in sesquiquadrate aspect (135 degrees) if they are within 3 degrees of each other. The symbol for the sesquiquadrate aspect is ⚟.

Planets which are six signs apart are in opposition aspect (180 degrees) if they are within 9 degrees of each other. The symbol for the opposition aspect is ☍.

Planets which are seven signs apart arc in sextile aspect (210 degrees—180 degrees plus 30 degrees) if they are within 3 degrees of each other.

Planets which are seven and a half signs apart are in semi-square aspect (225 degrees—180 degrees plus 45 degrees) if they are within 3 degrees of each other.

Planets which are 8 signs apart are in trine aspect (240 degrees) if they are within 5 degrees of each other.

Planets which are 9 signs apart are in square aspect (270 degrees) if they are within 5 degrees of each other.

Planets which are 10 signs apart are in sextile aspect (300 degrees) if they are within 5 degrees of each other.

Planets which are 11 signs apart are in semi-sextile aspect (330 degrees) if they are within 3 degrees of each other.

Planets which are 10 and a half signs apart are in sesquiquadrate aspect (315 degrees) if they are within 3 degrees of each other.

After the planets have been placed around the example Chart of the New York Stock Exchange for March 1938, several factors are noticeable (*see page 103*):

(1) The first factor is that the depressing planet Saturn is placed in the Midheaven or tenth house of the chart;

McWhirter Theory of Stock Market Forecasting

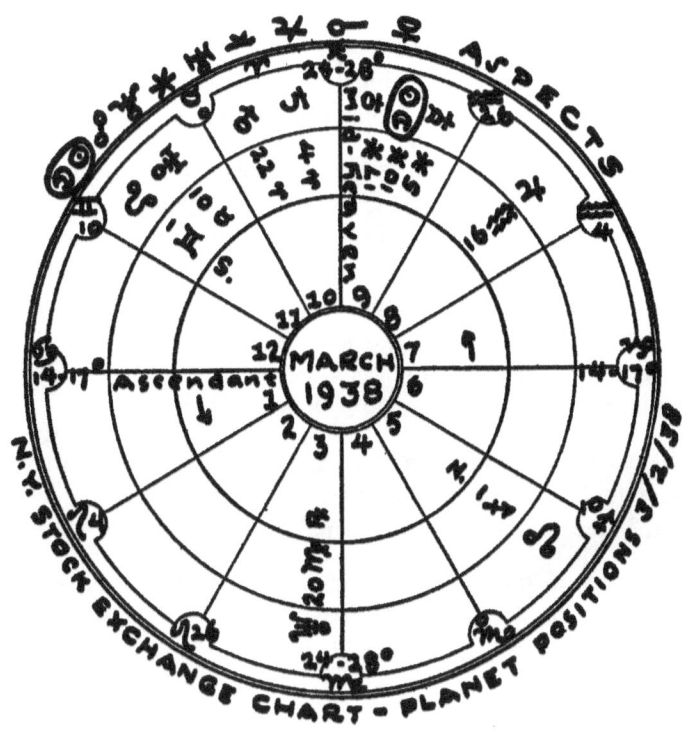

New York Stock Exchange Chart
Planetary Positions, March 2, 1938

This chart forecasts a downturn in the stock market
Aspects or angles in force at this lunation are:
Sun and Moon Opposition Neptune
Sun and Moon Sextile Uranus
Sun and Moon Semi-sextile Jupiter
Sun and Moon Conjunction Venus

(2) Mars, one of the planetary rulers of the Midheaven of the chart, is in the tenth house or Midheaven;

(3) The aspects in force at the lunation showed no aspects to either Mars or Saturn, but the lunation did show Neptune in opposition aspect to the lunation (conjunction of the Sun and Moon).

Neptune is one of the rulers of the Midheaven of the New York Stock Exchange Chart, and the fact that the lunation formed an unfavorable opposition aspect to it showed a slump in stock prices. Since the lunation made no aspect to either Mars or Saturn, their influence would not be brought into effect at this time. Unfavorable aspects to Neptune at a lunation, especially if no favorable aspect between Saturn and Uranus was in force at the same time, usually indicates a sharp break in stock market prices.

Saturn and Uranus, although one sign apart, were not in orb of aspect for a semi-sextile aspect because they were six degrees apart. Three degrees apart is the maximum orb for this aspect.

The conclusion reached through this method of forecasting the trend of the Stock Market was that prices were going lower at this time and that March might possibly witness a slump or sharp break during the month.

What actually happened, as any one can verify by reference to the newspapers for March, was that stocks went lower during the entire month, and on March 29, 1938, as the Moon passed over the degree of the lunation of March 2, 1938, the full force of the unfavorable aspect to Neptune was brought into play and stocks plunged downward in a selling wave that hit three-year lows. Stocks were at their 1932 level.

For an "example month" when an upturn in stock market prices was indicated (at the lunation occurring previous to the upturn) we will take the month of June 1938.

By turning to the ephemeris we see that a lunation, or New Moon, occurred on May 29, 1938, and on June 27, 1938. Since we want the lunation covering the month of June 1938, we will take the lunation of May 29, 1938. (The New Moon of June 27, 1938 would cover the month of July 1938.)

The planetary positions on May 29, 1938, were as follows: Sun 6 degrees Gemini; Moon 6 degrees Gemini; Neptune 18 degrees Virgo, retrograde; Uranus 15 degrees Taurus; Saturn 14 degrees Aries; Jupiter 1 degree Pisces; Mars 23 degrees Gemini; Venus 5 degrees Cancer; Mercury 13 degrees Taurus. The Moon's North Node was in 27 degrees Scorpio. Aspects in force at this lunation were Sun and Moon semi-square Saturn; square Jupiter; semi-sextile Venus.

When these planetary positions are placed around the New York Stock Exchange chart *(see page 106)*, we find three notable facts:

(1) The lunation (conjunction of the Sun and Moon every twenty-eight days) made no aspect to Neptune or Mars, the two planetary rulers of the New York Stock Exchange chart's Midheaven or tenth house;

(2) The two planets which point out major trends in the Stock Market, Saturn and Uranus, were in close semi-sextile aspect (30 degrees), which is favorable;

(3) At the same time Mercury was in conjunction with Uranus; and both Mercury and Uranus were in a very favorable trine (120 degrees) aspect with Neptune. Mercury also was in favorable semi-sextile aspect to the very powerful planet Saturn.

Favorable aspects between Saturn and Uranus always indicate an upturn in the stock market which will last as long as the aspect is in force. All aspects between Saturn and Uranus are very significant in studying stock market trends. The semi-sextile aspect did not come into effect between these two planets until they had become almost exact due to the fact that the semi-sextile aspect is only a minor favorable aspect and the orb of its influence does not extend beyond an area of three degrees (see the tabulation of aspects and their orb of influence listed in this chapter).

Monthly and Daily Trends on the New York Stock Exchange

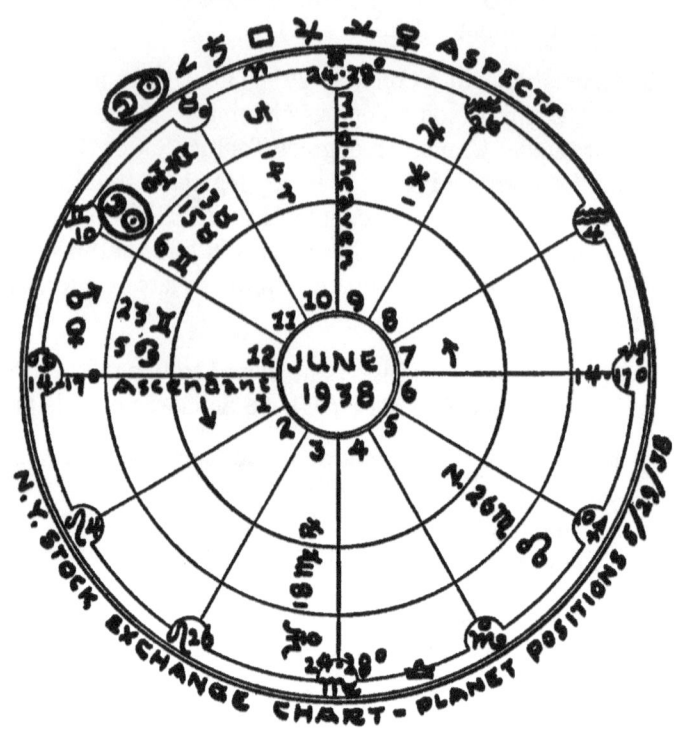

New York Stock Exchange Chart
Planetary Positions, May 29, 1938

This chart forecasts an upturn in the stock market.
Aspects or angles in force at this lunation are:
Sun and Moon Semi-square Saturn
Sun and Moon Square Jupiter
Sun and Moon Semi-sextile Venus

One fact should be pointed out here. Raphael's Ephemeris lists the lunation of May 29, 1938, as in semi-square aspect to Saturn. They allow large orbs of influence and in this work we allow only three degrees for a semi-square aspect orb; therefore, although listed as such in the Ephemeris the lunation did not actually form a semi-square aspect to Saturn unless wide orbs of influence are used, and these have not been found advisable in studying stock market trends.

Although the upturn in the stock market was indicated for the month of June, the rise did not begin until June 20, 1938. On this date the Moon was passing over the Midheaven of the New York Stock Exchange chart. It is a noticeable fact that when marked daily changes occur in the stock market, such as a sharp drop or a sharp rise, the Moon is usually in one of the angles of the New York Stock Exchange chart, that is in the signs Pisces, Aries, Cancer, Virgo, Libra, or Capricorn.

Mars is usually involved when there is an active stock market either for buying or selling. In this case we find that at the lunation of May 29, 1938, Mars was in 23 degrees Gemini and unaspected. Mercury which was in conjunction with Uranus and semi-sextile Saturn at the time of the lunation, reached 23-25 degrees Gemini, the place of Mars at the lunation over the weekend, and came into play in stock market action Monday, June 20, 1938. Mercury was the planet which acted to bring the lunation indications into force, since it was the planet which aspected Saturn, Uranus, and Neptune at the New Moon. If Saturn or Uranus had been strongly aspected by the lunation, the Moon's passage or the Sun's passage over 23-25 degrees Gemini, the place of Mars at the lunation, would have brought out the upturn in the stock market predicted May 29, 1938. This is further proof that the lunation was not in orb of a semi-square aspect with Saturn in so far as this work is concerned, even though it is listed in the Ephemeris as such. Wide orbs do not work in forecasting stock market conditions and none should be used except those given in this Chapter; otherwise your market forecasting will go sadly awry.

Monthly and Daily Trends on the New York Stock Exchange

Thus it is seen that the rise in the stock market averages was foretold by the fact that Saturn and Uranus came into favorable aspect with each other in June 1938. This fact was pointed out at the previous lunation of May 29, 1938, by Mercury being in conjunction with Uranus; both planets being in semi-sextile aspect to Saturn, a key planet, since it is placed on the Midheaven of the New York Stock Exchange chart; and both Mercury and Uranus being in very favorable trine aspect (120 *degrees*) with Neptune, one of the rulers of the Midheaven of the New York Stock Exchange Chart.

When Mercury reached the place of Mars, the other ruler of the Midheaven of the New York Stock Exchange Chart, and a planet usually involved in active stock market buying and selling, on Monday, June 20, 1938, the stock market rise began.

Aspects between Saturn and Uranus govern major bull and bear markets, as well as secondary rises and slumps, and this upturn in the stock market will last as long as the favorable aspect between Saturn and Uranus is in force. The semi-sextile aspect between Saturn and Uranus has just half the force of the sextile aspect (60 degrees) which existed between Saturn and Uranus from March 1933 and affected market conditions until August 1937. Traders should keep this fact in mind. The Dow-Jones Industrial Averages stood at 107.74 May 31, 1938, and by July 2, 1938, had risen to 138.53. With a little practice, anyone who studies the rules laid down in this chapter can forecast the major upturns and downturns in the stock market averages. The monthly and daily trends of the stock market are easily forecast through the method and rules laid down in this chapter. Like any other subject, practice, in analyzing market conditions through this method, makes for perfection and accuracy.

The rules laid down in this chapter are particularly applicable for studying the fluctuations in the Dow-Jones Market Averages.

This method of forecasting the trend of the stock market is in its infancy and offers unlimited possibilities for research and study.

For the first time in history, it offers a method for forecasting economic cycles years, months, and days in advance, which is based on natural law. The study of these rules will doubly repay anyone. It offers to the man with a small capital a chance for economic security. Above all, it teaches you when to get in and when to get out of the stock market.

All that is written in this book is not all there is to the subject. That would require many books to contain so vast an amount of economic history. It is, however, an attempt to place economic security within the reach of all through a method of planned investment and economic research.

No one can account for slumps and booms in reality. Any number of reasons are given out *after* the condition occurs, explaining its reason for happening. This is all right as far as it goes, but our theory goes further because it tells you in advance how to prevent the manifestation of an undesirable economic condition. Extremes are not desirable. Booms are inevitably followed by depression and human suffering. This book points out a way for a more stable national security.

Monthly and Daily Trends on the New York Stock Exchange

Chapter IV

How to Forecast Trends of Individual Stocks

Nothing would be more advantageous to the average trader than a simplified method whereby he or she could tell at a glance the future possibilities of a stock for investment purposes. This chapter offers such a system based on the transits of the major planets (Jupiter, Saturn, Uranus, Neptune, and Pluto) in aspect to the Sun, Moon, and planetary ruler of the sign under which the stock was incorporated. (*The twelve signs of the zodiac and their planetary rulers are given in Chapter III.*) Usually the trends of most stocks (either up, down or steady) conforms to the general trend of the Stock Market, but there are always some stocks which move opposite to the general trend and it is very important to know these stocks to avoid tying up money in a company which is not going to show profit. Secondly, everyone wants to know when a stock has reached a low buying level and the only way this information can be obtained is by studying the stock individually and noting what the stock has done in the past. Chapter V gives the date and place of incorporation of every important stock listed at the present time on the New York Stock Exchange. It is a simple matter to work out the planetary positions from the date and place of incorporation and to then set these planetary positions around a

How to Forecast Trends of Individual Stocks

chart as in Example I, the chart of U.S. Steel, and find out by studying the transits to the planetary positions of the stock in question what it offers in the way of profitable investment for the future.

The best way to learn how to forecast the future possibilities of a stock is to take a stock as an example and go through the process. By repeating the process several times, it becomes an easy matter to tell what any stock will do in the next twelve years.

As Example I, let us take U.S. Steel (X). To be able to forecast this stock is important for several reasons. It is the leading stock of the Steel industry and any move made by this company is always regarded significantly by the business and financial world. During the September and October 1937 slumps, U.S. Steel and the general trend of the Stock Market moved so similarly that an investigating committee, probing the cause of the slumps, studied the trading volume of U.S. Steel exclusively. Dividends paid by this company are always watched closely as indications of future market action. In order to study this important stock according to the transit method of this chapter, it is necessary to know its planetary positions, which are given in Chapter V.

The list of stocks, arranged alphabetically in Chapter V, giving the planetary positions of some important stocks listed on the New York Stock Exchange, follows the order of stocks listed on the "Big Board" which appear daily in the newspapers. The planetary positions of a stock are obtained from its incorporation date, if this is known; otherwise, from its date of establishment or organization date.

In order to find the planetary positions of U.S. Steel, we turn to Chapter V and run down the alphabet until we come to the stock listing:

U.S. Steel (X) incorporated February 23, 1901, in New Jersey. Sun 4 degrees Pisces; Moon 4 degrees Taurus; Neptune 26 degrees Gemini Retrograde; Uranus 16 degrees Sagittarius; Saturn 13 degrees Capricorn; Jupiter 6 degrees Capricorn; Mars 2 degrees

McWhirter Theory of Stock Market Forecasting

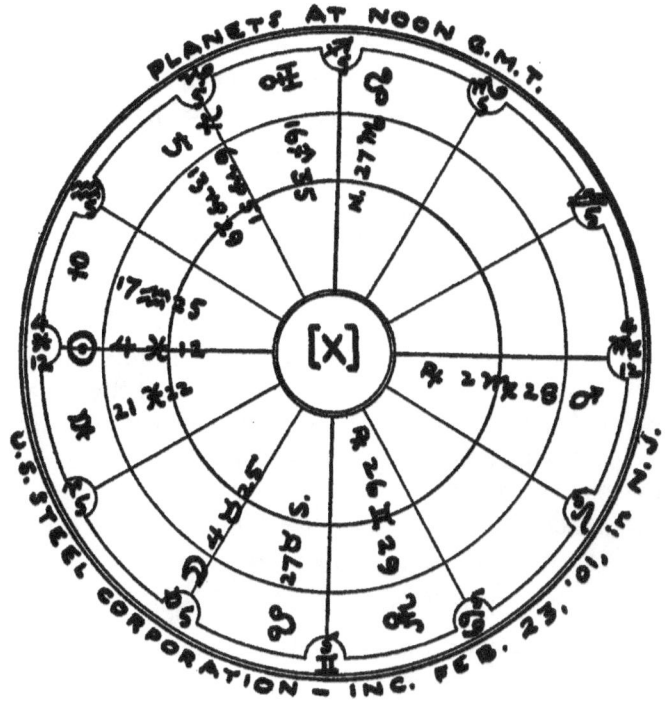

Example I, The United States Steel Corporation Chart Incorporated February 23, 1901 in New Jersey.

Virgo Retrograde; Venus 17 degrees Aquarius; Mercury 21 degrees Pisces; the Moon's North Node 27 degrees Scorpio.

The next step is to place these planetary positions on a chart or wheel as in Example I. The Sun's degree is placed on the Ascendant or first house with the Sun on the cusp of the first house. The other eleven cusps of the chart take the next degree, which in this case is 5, and the signs follow in their natural order until there is a sign on all the cusps of the chart. The Sun's degree was 4 Pisces in the case of U.S. Steel. The sign following Pisces is Aries and it carries the figure 5 to show 5 degrees Aries; the sign which normally follows Aries in the zodiac is Taurus, and Taurus 5 degrees is placed on the third cusp. The sign which follows Taurus in the zodiac is Gemini and the symbol for Gemini 5 degrees is put on the cusp of the fourth house; and so forth around the chart, until there is a sign on each of the twelve cusps or houses of the chart. (*The order of the twelve signs of the zodiac with their symbols is given in Chapter III.*)

The other nine planets are filled in on the chart in their proper houses or positions.

According to the list of planetary positions for U.S. Steel the Moon is 4 degrees Taurus. Since Taurus (♉) 5 degrees falls on the cusp of the second house, the Moon (☽) would fall slightly above the second house. Remember the signs and planets are arranged counter-clockwise on the chart. Symbols for the signs and planets are used on the chart and these symbols are given in Chapter III. It is much easier and simpler to use the symbols for the signs and planets instead of writing them out.

Neptune (♆) falls in 26 degrees Gemini (♊), in the list of this Company's planetary positions. Since 5 degrees Gemini falls on the cusp of the fourth house and 5 degrees Cancer is on the cusp of the fifth house, 26 degrees Gemini comes between these two points and Neptune is placed in the fourth house. Neptune is listed retrograde (Rx) in the list and this means that while the other planets are moving direct in motion or counter-clockwise at the time this stock was incorporated, Neptune was moving backwards in its orbit or in clockwise motion. Retrograde planets do not seem to have as strong an influence in a chart as planets which are moving in direct motion. The Sun and Moon are always direct in motion, never retrograde; therefore, their positions are always important when analyzing a stock's future. In the list of those planetary positions given in Chapter V, those stocks incorporated or organized from 1850 to 1930 have their positions given in terms of Greenwich Mean Time Noon. Those stocks listed as being incorporated from 1931 until the present date have their planetary positions given in terms of Greenwich Mean Time midnight. This fact is mentioned for those individuals interested in working out the minutes on the degrees listed. For the average trader the minutes are not important and therefore they have been omitted from the planetary examples listed for the stocks in Chapter V. For analyzing the future outlook for any stock the degrees of the planets are all that is needed, since hour of incorporation is not known for many stocks, and the transit method seems to work better when using the simple outline given in the examples listed in this Chapter.

The next planet in the list to be placed on the chart is Uranus (♅), which is in 16 degrees Sagittarius (♐). 5 degrees Sagittarius falls on the tenth house cusp and 5 degrees Capricorn on the eleventh house cusp. Thus 16 degrees Sagittarius falls between these two points and therefore Uranus is placed in the tenth house.

Saturn (♄) is 13 degrees Capricorn (♑) and this point falls between the eleventh and twelfth house on the chart since 5 degrees Capricorn is on the eleventh house cusp and 5 degrees Aquarius is on the twelfth house cusp.

Jupiter (♃) is 6 degrees Capricorn (♑) and this point falls right under the eleventh house cusp.

Mars (♂) is 2 degrees Virgo (♍). This planet is marked by the Retrograde symbol (Rx) because it was moving backward in its orbit at the time this stock was incorporated. 2 degrees Virgo falls between 5 degrees Leo and 5 degrees Virgo; therefore, Mars should be placed just under the seventh house cusp. Usually the same degree (in this case 4) is put on the seventh house cusp which the Sun carries. Either 4 or 5 is alright.

Venus (♀) is 17 degrees Aquarius (♒) and this point falls between 5 degrees Aquarius and 4 degrees Pisces; therefore, it is placed in the twelfth house.

Mercury (☿) is 21 degrees Pisces (♓) and falls between 4 degrees Pisces and 5 degrees Aries; it is, therefore, put in the first house. The Moon's North Node (☊) is 27 degrees Scorpio (♏)

and this point falls between 5 degrees Scorpio and 5 degrees Sagittarius. The Moon's North Node is therefore placed in the ninth house. The Moon's South Node (☋) falls exactly opposite this point in the opposite sign of the zodiac. It is therefore put in the third house in 27 degrees Taurus. These important points are always noted as they often give a clue as to whether the stock would work with the general trend of the stock market and business cycle or against it in its own general cycle. In the case of U.S. Steel we see that this stock would move along basically with the general trend of business and the stock market due to the fact that Scorpio is the sign on the Business Cycle Chart marking the transition point from normal to above normal business activity; and Taurus is the sign on the Business Cycle Chart which marks the transition point from normal business activity to below normal business volume and economic conditions. (*For a copy of the Business Cycle Chart as originated by the writer, see Chapter I.*)

The North Node has an expansive influence similar to Jupiter. The South Node has a restrictive influence similar to Saturn. In the list of planetary positions of leading stocks given in Chapter V the North Node only is given because the South Node always carries the same degree as the North Node in the sign exactly opposite (180 degrees away) from the sign in which the North Node is placed. The signs of the zodiac and their sign opposites are:

Aries	Libra
Taurus	Scorpio
Gemini	Sagittarius
Cancer	Capricorn
Leo	Aquarius
Virgo	Pisces

There are a number of stocks listed on the New York Stock Exchange which work against the general trend of the stock market due to their own individual stock cycles. It is a comparatively easy matter to know how any stock's cycle is related to the business cycle or general trend of the stock market by simply noting the Node positions of a stock and then comparing these signs positions with the Business Cycle Chart.

In the case of U.S. Steel it is easy to see that this stock would move with the general trend of business and the general trend of the stock market. As a proof of this (which took place recently), last September (1937) stocks slumped and the business curve turned downward. U.S. Steel broke during the slump from 104.5 to 80.5. The New York Stock Exchange sent out a questionnaire to all Exchange members and member firms to get information on this stock's buying and selling in order to find out what was back of the market slump. They explained that this stock was selected because as U.S. Steel had gone so had gone the stock market!

Another fact concerning this stock is that it is incorporated under the sign of Pisces, which is the sign on the Midheaven of the New York Stock Exchange Chart. (*For a copy of this Chart see Chapter III.*) This shows a further tie-up between U.S. Steel's trend and the trend of the stock market. Planetary transits through Pisces or in aspect to Pisces would naturally affect the trend of the stock market and the trend of U.S. Steel similarly. From 1935 to 1937 Saturn was passing through the sign of Pisces. Uranus was in favorable aspect to Saturn until 1937 and U.S. Steel rose with the stock market consistently, breaking only in April 1937, and in September and October 1937, during the market breaks at that time. In 1935 U.S. Steel had a deficit of $2.77 per share. During 1936 earnings amounted to $2.90 per share and the stock sold between 15.99 and 27.54 times its earnings. During 1937 the earnings of U.S. Steel amounted to $8.01 per share with the stock selling between 6.05 and 15.79 times its earnings. This compared with 1929, when the earnings of this stock amounted to $21.19 per share and the stock sold between 7.08 and 12.35 times its earnings. In 1920, the epoch-making planet Uranus went into the sign of Pisces and did not leave this sign until 1927. This passage of Uranus out of Pisces culminated in the forming of new stock for U.S. Steel.

How to Forecast Trends of Individual Stocks

After the planetary positions of a stock have been placed around a chart in their proper positions, the next and most important step is to study out the future investment possibilities of the stock from the chart thus set up. (All stocks have their charts set up in exactly the same manner as U.S. Steel, the example used here in this analysis.)

The Sun (☉) in any chart stands for the company; and has to do with the organization, management and aims of the company; the officers, and products of the firm. The Sun, and the planetary aspects to the Sun, both at the incorporation date, and at any future time, clearly point out the profit possibilities of the stock. The position of the Sun in any stock's chart is the most important planetary position to be considered and for this reason the Sun is placed on the Ascendant of the stock's chart and the other planets placed in relation to it. This is logical, for it is a well known fact that the organization and management of a company determine its financial success. I have noticed that when the Sun is badly aspected at the time of incorporation, the Company has to merge later with another company or has to go out of business completely. Aspects to the Sun are of paramount importance, both at the time of incorporation and at a later date by transit of the major planets to the Sun.

The Moon (☽) stands for the public; the buying public and the attitude of the people toward the company or to its products. Aspects to the Moon are important and second only to the Sun. Regardless of how good a concern is, there must be a demand for the goods produced and a buying public. A company which is incorporated at a time when the Moon is in favorable aspect to the Sun lasts a long time and is usually most successful. In the case of U.S. Steel we find that the Moon is placed in a favorable sextile (60 *degrees*) aspect to the Sun. This is an excellent sign for continuation of this company for many years to come. It has already been in existence thirty-seven years. This is a long time in view of the fact that many companies which were listed on the New York Stock Exchange only three years ago have long been out of existence. Companies are organized and go out of business overnight!

Jupiter (♃) stands for the money-making possibilities of a company. It shows the money behind a company and its chances for expansion. In the case of U.S. Steel, Jupiter is in 6 degrees Capricorn in favorable sextile (60 *degrees*) aspect with the Sun (company) and in very favorable trine aspect (120 *degrees*) with the Moon (Public). It is therefore, easy to surmise that U.S. Steel would make money and also would be a very popular stock with the trading public.

Saturn (♄) stands for the limitations of the company and usually when Saturn is placed in unfavorable aspect to the Sun or Moon at the time of incorporation, the company has many vicissitudes in a financial way. Whenever Saturn by transit moves in unfavorable aspect to the Sun, and in a lesser degree to the Moon, it usually is a bad year for a company. Therefore, make it a rule never to invest in a stock when Saturn by transit is unfavorably aspecting the Sun or Moon in a chart. You will find that you will tie up your money or suffer loss by having the stock go down on you.

Mars (♂) governs the activity of a stock. Whenever Mars at the time of incorporation or by transit strongly aspects the Sun, Moon, Jupiter, or its own place at the time of incorporation, the stock will fluctuate strongly while under the stimuli of Mars. Other aspects in force at the time of the Mars transit determine whether the stock will move up or down or just back-and-fill for the time being. Always look to see whether a stock is temporarily under a Mars aspect if it starts moving in a very active manner. Unless there are other testimonies present which indicate that the stock is on an up trend, do not rush and buy a stock, because it suddenly becomes active. Aspects from Mars pass very quickly and you may find your funds later or in a short time tied up in an inactive stock. In the case of U.S. Steel, our example stock. Mars is in favorable trine aspect to Jupiter and the Moon. It is in an opposition aspect to the Sun. This would be unfavorable if Mars were not in favorable aspect to Jupiter and the Moon, which in turn are in favorable aspect to the Sun, as well as being in favorable aspect to each other! This is a very strong favorable planetary tie-up and not only shows an active stock, but an extremely strong Company with enlarged powers.

Another noticeable fact about U.S. Steel should be brought out here. The steel stocks as a group come under the rulership of the earth and water signs, that is the signs of Taurus, Virgo, Capricorn, Cancer, Scorpio, and Pisces, and U.S. Steel certainly bears out this fact with every important planet in earth and water signs. The Sun is in Pisces, a water sign, and the Moon, Jupiter, Mars, and Saturn are in earth signs. Stability is certainly shown here for this company with so many planets in earth signs.

It is well to know what the various sign rulerships of the main groups of stocks on the New York Stock Exchange are. Whenever the Sun or other major planets pass through these signs, stocks which fall under these groups are stimulated to activity. This accounts for the seasonal popularity of certain groups of stocks which can be accounted for in no other way. Often it is possible to trade in a certain group of stocks for a month and make money when other groups are unaccentuated. For instance, the aviation group comes under the rulership mainly of the fire signs, that is Aries, Leo, and Sagittarius, with Sagittarius particularly strong. December (and usually the latter part of November) is a good time to trade in aviation stocks for they are nearly always active at this time. During December 1935, 1936, and 1937, the aircraft issues were strong and active. This was particularly so in 1935, when Jupiter, the planet of expansion, moved into Sagittarius for a year's stay. It is interesting to note in connection with the strong affinity between aviation stocks and the sign Sagittarius that in the natural order of the signs of the zodiac Sagittarius rules the ninth house, which has to do with distant places, long trips, and traveling.

The chemical stocks come under the rulership of the fire signs; and as a rule, so do many of the railroad stocks.

The oil stocks come mainly under the influence of the air signs, particularly the sign of Libra. The other two air signs are Gemini and Aquarius.

Utilities come under a combination of water and earth signs. July is often a good month for utilities and steel and so is January, the latter part of February, and November. These months do not always hold good due to the fact that there may be present other major planets which counteract this seasonal stimulation; however, it is well to know when certain groups will be active. Oils are usually good in September and October of each year or at least very active.

In studying the chart of a stock, one other planetary factor must be taken into account and that is the planet which rules the sign the Sun is placed in, or in other words, the sign under which the stock is incorporated. In the case of U.S. Steel, the Sun is in Pisces, and the ruler of Pisces is Neptune, which in this company's chart is placed in 26 degrees Gemini. Aspects to Neptune will often give a clue to the change in trend of this stock when other testimonies are lacking. Therefore, before making any final judgment on what a stock will or will not do in the future, always take into consideration any aspects to the stock's planetary ruler. This is always the planet which rules the sign in which the Sun is placed. (*For a list of the twelve signs and their planetary rulers see Chapter III.*)

The following transits influence a stock's future trend: the trend will be upward if Jupiter and Uranus are placed in a favorable aspect to the Sun, that is forming angles of 0, 60, or 120 degrees.

The trend will be downward if Saturn or Uranus is placed in unfavorable aspect to the Sun or Moon in the company's chart, that is, forming angles of 90 degrees, 180, 135, and in the case of Saturn, in 0 degrees or conjunction aspect. Do not invest in a stock which is under an unfavorable aspect to the Sun or Moon. Always invest in a stock which is coming under a favorable aspect from Jupiter or Uranus singly or when both planets ace placed in favorable aspect to each other and are aspecting the Sun or Moon of a company. If the major planets Saturn and Uranus are in favorable aspect to each other and they aspect the Sun or Moon in a company's chart, this is also a good time to invest in a stock. If Saturn and Uranus are in unfavorable aspect to each other as transits and one of the planets, or both, aspect the Sun and Moon in a company's chart, the trend will be decidedly downward and to invest in it would bring financial loss.

In the case of U.S. Steel, Saturn moved into Pisces in March 1935, and this was an unfavorable influence, but at the same time the major planet Uranus formed a favorable sextile aspect with transiting Saturn and at the same time was in conjunction with the Moon in the chart of U.S. Steel and in a very favorable trine aspect to Jupiter and Mars in the chart besides being in favorable aspect to the Sun. In the face of such testimony, even a rank amateur in judgment could not conclude anything else but the fact that U.S. Steel was going up and that it was an excellent investment possibility. This is all the more true in view of the fact that a favorable aspect between Saturn and Uranus usually marks an upturn in the stock market. Anyone who could have studied the possibilities ahead for U.S. Steel in this simple manner would have been able to make a fortune. However, how was a trader to know how long this upturn would last? In view of the fact that U. S. Steel moves with the stock market generally, it was a safe estimate that this stock would go up as long as the stock market pointed upward, which would be relatively the time during which Saturn and Uranus were in favorable aspect. This was from 1935 to 1937. In March 1935, this stock was as low as $30.00 per share; in March 1937, it had risen to between $125.00 to $130.00 per share. This stock dropped to $40.00 by the spring of 1938. It is again at a buying level. Why?

During 1939, Jupiter will be in the sign of Pisces, and at the same time will go over the Midheaven of the New York Stock Exchange. It is logical to conclude that this stock is going to rise and therefore, it is a good investment proposition for 1939, since it is ruled by Pisces.

During 1939, Jupiter will pass through Pisces, the sign under which U.S. Steel is incorporated and this stock should rise during the coming year. During 1939, transiting Uranus will be in favorable aspect to Jupiter during the spring months especially and this is added planetary strength indicating that this stock will go up.

All stocks are studied in the same manner as U.S. Steel. It is always necessary to set up a chart as has been done in the case of this stock and study the planetary relationships and aspects of the company involved. Then in order to know whether the stock is good for investment purposes for the future, it is necessary to study its Node positions in order to ascertain whether the stock would work with the general trend of the stock market. The next and last step is to determine the planetary aspects for any future year which are formed by the transiting planets to the Sun and Moon in the chart of the stock. With a little practice, it becomes a simple matter to know whether a stock would be a wise investment at any particular time. Naturally, as with any other subject, the more familiar you become with this method of studying a stock's investment possibilities the more accurate you become in your analysis of that stock.

As an example of a stock which offered tremendous possibilities for profit within a space of five years and which probably nobody invested in, it is interesting to study the chart of Spiegel, Inc. (SMS), formerly Spiegel-May-Stern Co. This stock was incorporated April 28, 1928, in Delaware. Its planetary positions are given in Chapter V, as follows: Sun 7 degrees Taurus; Moon 27 degrees Leo; Neptune 26 degrees Leo, Retrograde; Uranus 5 degrees Aries; Saturn 8 degrees Sagittarius, Retrograde; Jupiter 21 degrees Aries; Venus 20 degrees Aries; Mercury 2 degrees Taurus; the Moon's North Node 11 degrees Gemini.

The chart of this company is set up in exactly the same manner as the chart of U.S. Steel. The Sun is placed on the Ascendant with its degree, that is 7 degrees Taurus. The remaining eleven houses have the remaining eleven signs of the zodiac placed around the chart in their proper order with 8 degrees equally placed on the eleven house cusps. The planets are then put in their proper houses, depending, of course, for their positions on the degree of the sign which they carry. (*See Example II on page 124.*)

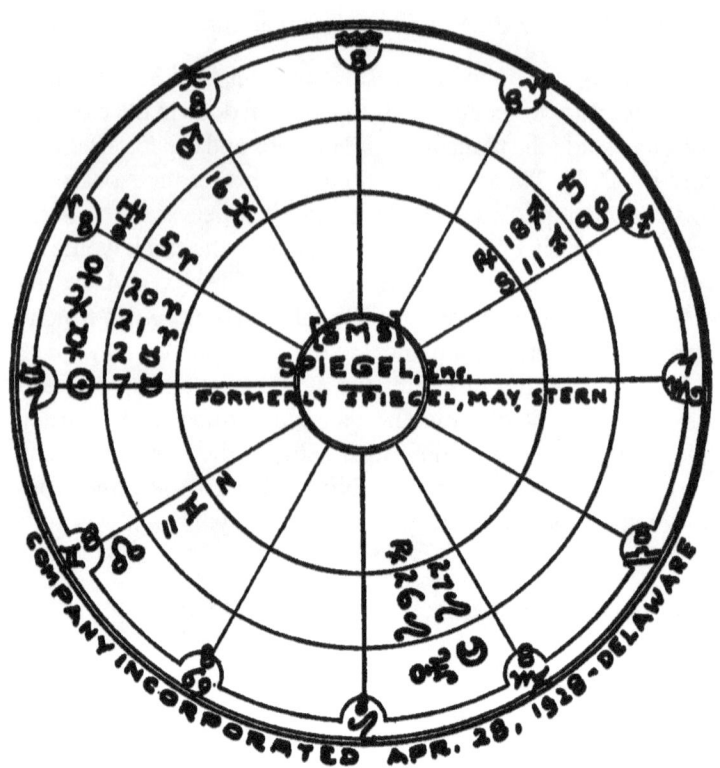

Example II, Spiegel, Inc.
(Formerly Spiegel, May, Stern)
Chart revealing tremendous money-making possibilities.

In May 1932, the stock of Spiegel, May, Stern Co. sold for 62½ cents per share. For the sum of $500.00, 800 shares of SMS could have been bought. By December 1936, the stock's value had climbed to $114.30 per share. If this stock had been purchased in May 1932, for 62½ cents per share and 800 shares had been bought, these 800 shares would have been worth $91,600.00! In five years time another opportunity for sound investment had passed and probably there are very few people who took advantage of it.

What in this company's chart showed that it would have such phenomenal money-making possibilities? A study of this company's chart reveals much.

It is a well known fact in this method of studying a stock's future that a chart which shows the Sun, which is symbolic of the company, under unfavorable aspects at the time of the incorporation has very little chance of making money. The same rule holds true for the Moon in a lesser degree. The Moon is symbolic of the Public; the public buying interest and the attitude of the masses toward the product for sale. If the Moon is badly aspected at the time of incorporation, the company works under a heavy handicap and more often than not eventually has to go out of business.

In the chart of Spiegel, Inc. the Sun (company) is in favorable semi-sextile aspect with the epoch-making planet Uranus. Mercury is in conjunction with the Sun, giving added trading strength. Uranus is also in favorable semi-sextile aspect to Mercury. The Moon (public) is in conjunction with Neptune and in very favorable trine aspect to both Venus and Jupiter (financial possibilities), Venus and Jupiter are in conjunction with each other in Aries. The limitations of the company are shown by Saturn's position and aspects. This planet in the chart of SMS is in very favorable trine aspect to Jupiter (money-making possibilities of the company). Mars ruling the activity of the stock is in favorable semi-sextile aspect to Jupiter and Venus. It is in unfavorable square aspect to Saturn, but since Saturn is trine Jupiter (financial gain), this aspect between Mars and Saturn is not as forceful as it otherwise would be, if both planets were not favorably aspecting the money-making planet Jupiter.

Therefore, it is easy to conclude that this stock was a good investment. The Sun, Moon, Jupiter, and even restrictive Saturn were in favorable aspect at the time of incorporation. After this stock was incorporated, it did not immediately go up. There were no major transiting aspects present to bring out the latent possibilities of the good chart. In 1932, the epoch-making Uranus, which

How to Forecast Trends of Individual Stocks

was favorably aspecting the Sun (company) at the time of incorporation, moved into conjunction with Jupiter and Venus in Aries, forming at the same time a very favorable trine aspect with the Moon (public) and Neptune in Leo. This started the upturn which continued upward sharply from 1934 through 1936 when Uranus moved through the first 10 degrees of Taurus and over the Sun's degree of 7 Taurus.

To know whether this stock is a good buy for the future, or whether *any stock* is a good investment for the future, it is necessary to study the transits of the major planets which will aspect the Sun, Moon, and Jupiter at that time. In the case of this stock (SMS), transiting Jupiter will be in favorable sextile aspect during the first two months of 1939. This is due to the fact that Jupiter will be in Pisces at this time and passing through the first 10 degrees or decanate of Pisces. Pisces forms a sextile aspect with the sign Taurus and planets passing through the first 10 degrees of Pisces would be in favorable sextile aspect to the Sun in this company's chart, which is in 7 degrees Taurus. This is favorable for gains. During the summer months of 1939, Jupiter will move into Aries and will pass through the first 10 degrees of the sign. In this position transiting Jupiter will form a conjunction aspect with Uranus and a semi-sextile aspect with the Sun. This is a favorable indication.

During all of 1939, Saturn will be passing through the third decanate (or 20 to 30 degrees) Aries. In this position, transiting Saturn will exert a conservative influence over the financial gains of this company. Saturn's influence is always to limit, curb, and restrain unless it is under very favorable aspects from transiting Uranus at the same time. Saturn passing through the last 10 degrees of Aries forms a conjunction aspect with Jupiter and Venus, and a trine aspect with the Moon and Neptune.

During 1940, both Jupiter and Saturn will transit the sign of Taurus and in this position will pass over the Sun of this company. This is a mixed indication for the gains of this company, but in view of the fact that the Sun was well aspected at the time of incorporation, this stock should go upward.

Every chart, like every individual, has similar characteristics, but always there will be present a new set of conditions not present in the other. It takes time and practice to become adept in analyzing the charts of stocks, but it is interesting and very worthwhile because it helps you to obtain financial independence through investment of a sound and practical nature. The more time you give to this subject the more money you will be able to make. There is no method except the theory propounded in this book which offers such a quick and accurate analysis of individual stocks for the average person in the street who has a small capital to invest.

The positions of the transiting planets for every month during the next twelve years are given in any ephemeris (available from the American Federation of Astrologers). The incorporation date of every important stock listed on the New York Stock Exchange (as of July 1, 1938), with its planetary positions for that date, are given in Chapter V. Charts for each and every one of the stocks listed should be set up in the same way as the three charts for the three stocks used as examples in this chapter. They are analyzed in the same way. The first step, after setting up the chart correctly, is to study the planetary aspects present in the chart, particularly those to the Sun, Moon, and Jupiter. This gives the clue to the long life of the company; its relationship with the consuming public; and its money-making possibilities. The position and aspects to Saturn show the setbacks financially and otherwise which the company is apt to experience. Mars shows its strength and activity on the market.

The second step is to refer to the ephemeris and see when the major planets Uranus, Saturn, Jupiter, and Neptune aspect important planetary positions in the chart. This will give you the clue to when a big up or down movement will take place in the stock. When you are studying a stock and you find it is under no major planetary aspects for that period, then you are safe in judging that it will be in a sideways movement until it comes under major planetary aspects, and that to tie up money in the stock will bring you little or no financial returns. Invest in stocks which you know are coming under favorable planetary aspects only. Spiegel, Inc. (SMS), the stock used for Example II, is a good example of a stock which was coming under favorable aspects for several years to come and whose favorable indications for the future were dearly pointed out by its chart several years in advance.

If you have your capital invested in a stock whose chart clearly shows that it is coming under unfavorable transiting aspects, the thing to do is to find a chart of a stock which is coming under favorable aspects and buy in the stock favorably aspected. There is no virtue in holding a stock which is not making money for you.

It is interesting to study the chart of Sears Roebuck Co. (S), which was incorporated June 16, 1906, in New York. The planetary positions for this stock, which are given in Chapter V, are as follows: Sun 24 degrees Gemini; Moon 24 degrees Aries; Neptune 9 degrees Cancer; Uranus 7 degrees Capricorn; Saturn 14 degrees Pisces; Jupiter 20 degrees Gemini; Mars 3 degrees Cancer; Venus 25 degrees Cancer; Mercury 3 degrees Cancer. The Moon's North Node is 14 degrees Leo. This chart illustrates the enormous merchandising concern it represents.

That this company would be in existence a long time is shown by the fact that the Sun (company) is in a very favorable sextile (60 *degrees*) aspect with the Moon (public) besides being in conjunction with the money-making planet Jupiter. Jupiter (financial possibilities) was in favorable sextile aspect with the Moon (public). Venus, which has to do with clothes, cosmetics, or any items which have to do with women and children, was in semi-sextile aspect to both the Sun and Jupiter. Mars, which has to do with the activity of the company and stock, and the planet which sometimes shows the application of the company's interests, is in conjunction with Mercury (the mail) and Neptune (selling). Neptune also represents dealings which never actually contact a person face to face.

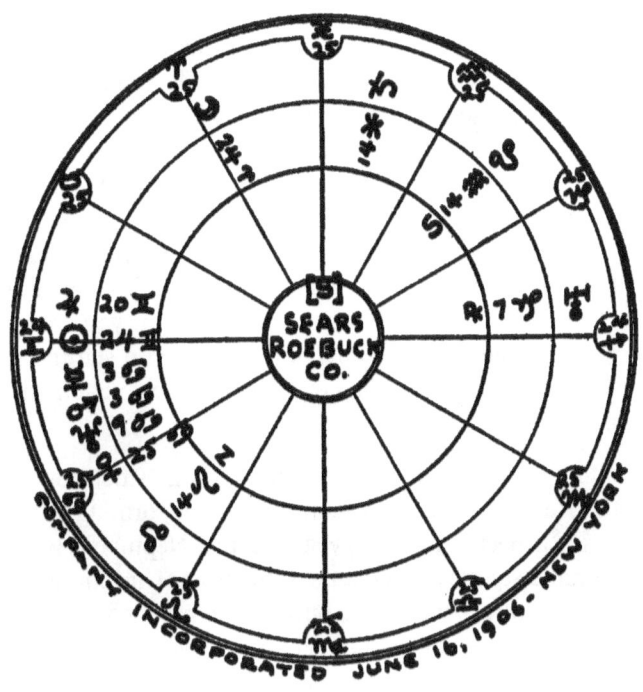

Example III
Sears Roebuck Company Chart
This chart shows unusual permanency factors.

Then again the sign of Cancer rules the home, and everything which has to do with the home, and there are four planets out of the nine in that sign. It would be easy to judge that this company has something to do with merchandise that is in some way connected with the home. It often happens that you can judge the kind of business a company is in by studying the planetary positions in force at the time it was incorporated. Sears Roebuck Co. is an excellent stock to study from its chart as it reveals much about the company which otherwise would never be known from a set of statistics concerning the company and its assets.

How to Forecast Trends of Individual Stocks

The chart of Sears Roebuck Co. is set up in the same way as the two other stocks used as examples in this chapter. The Sun in 24 degrees Gemini is placed on the Ascendant The remaining eleven signs follow in consecutive order and carry 25 degrees, except the seventh sign of Sagittarius, which carries the 24th degree. (The sign which falls on the seventh house opposite the Ascendant always carries the same degree as the Ascendant or first house). The planets are then placed around the chart in their proper places. A copy of the chart correctly set up accompanies this chapter and is marked "Example III." It would be a good idea, if you are not familiar with the setting up of charts, to practice on setting up the three example charts in this chapter to familiarize yourself with the process.

By studying the major transits affecting this stock for investment purposes, for 1938, we see that Jupiter is forming a very favorable trine aspect during this year, but that Neptune is placed in an unfavorable square aspect at the same time. This configuration represents two forces which are pulling against each other. Gains should predominate, but trading caution is advised before investing. During 1939, both Jupiter and Neptune will be unfavorably placed to the Sun and Jupiter in this company's stock. Careful study of the chart and actual movements of Sears Roebuck should be studied before buying during 1939.

It often happens that transiting Mars, which moves very quickly through the zodiac, aspects Jupiter or Mars, in a stock's chart, and during the transit the stock becomes very active. Do not be misled by this sudden activity of a stock, for as soon as the Mars aspect passes, the stock is apt to resume its former position or else, if it is not aspected by any major planets at the time, to then lapse into inactivity.

The forecasts for the example stocks are intended to be used as guides on how to forecast future trends of a stock. They are not intended to be buying and selling information. The only way to learn how to forecast the future trends of stocks, according to this method, is to work out examples in real life. We learn by actually doing a thing—not by reading pages of theory. The analyses of the three stocks are also intended for study purposes only. The three stocks chosen were picked for no particular financial reason, but were chosen at random from the list in Chapter V, merely because they would illustrate the points brought out in this chapter on how to forecast the trends of individual stocks.

When applying the transits to the chart of the stocks, if the reader is not familiar with aspects, favorable and unfavorable, he or she should study Chapter III and also Aspects in the Glossary. It is absolutely necessary to be familiar with the angular relationships existing between the planets at the time a company was incorporated, and also to know how to tell at a glance from the ephemeris whether a planet is forming an aspect of importance to the Sun, Moon, Jupiter, and Saturn in a company's chart, at any given time. It is also necessary to know the order of the signs of the zodiac in order to be able to place them correctly around the chart.

Blank charts for erecting the charts of stocks may be quickly drawn off on a blank sheet of paper from the ones shown in this book or a prepared pad may be purchased from the American Federation of Astrologers. Anyone can learn this method of forecasting the trend of stocks in a short time if he or she is willing to learn a few simple principles and apply them.

How to Forecast Trends of Individual Stocks

Chapter V

Date and Place of Incorporation of Stocks Listed on the New York Stock Exchange

Abraham and Strauss (AST). Incorporated January 19, 1920. Sun 28 degrees Capricorn; Moon 8 degrees Capricorn; Neptune 10 degrees Leo (retrograde); Uranus 29 degrees Aquarius; Saturn 11 degrees Virgo (retrograde); Jupiter 15 degrees Leo (retrograde); Mars 23 degrees Libra; Venus 17 degrees Sagittarius; Mercury 17 degrees Capricorn; the North Node 21 degrees Scorpio.

Adams Express Co. (AE). Incorporated July 1, 1854. Sun 9 degrees Cancer; Moon 15 degrees Virgo; Neptune 15 degrees Pisces; Uranus 15 degrees Taurus; Saturn 9 degrees Gemini; Jupiter 24 degrees Capricorn; Mars 25 degrees Virgo; Venus 29 degrees Taurus; Mercury 5 degrees Leo; Moon's North Node 29 degrees Taurus.

Addressograph Multigraph (AIN). Incorporated May 6, 1931 in Delaware.

Advance Runely Co. (RX). Reorganized February 9, 1931 in Indiana.

Affiliated Products (AFP). Incorporated June 26, 1930 in Delaware.

Stocks Listed on The New York Stock Exchange

Air Reduction Co. (AND). Incorporated November 26, 1915 in New York.

Airway Electrical Appliance (AWY). Incorporated July 23, 1920. Sun 0 degrees Leo; Moon 8 degrees Scorpio; Neptune 10 degrees Leo; Uranus 4 degrees Pisces Retrograde; Saturn 9 degrees Virgo; Jupiter 22 degrees Leo; Man 9 degrees Scorpio; Venus 5 degrees Leo; Mercury 6 degrees Leo; the Moon's North Node in the chart of this company is in 11 degrees of Scorpio.

Alaska Juneau Gold Mining Co. (AJ). Incorporated February 17, 1897 in West Virginia.

Albany and Susquehanna Railroad (AQS). Incorporated April 19, 1851 in New York.

Alleghany Corporation (Y). Incorporated January 26, 1929 in Maryland.

Alleghany Steel Co. (AGL). Incorporated May 6, 1929 in Pennsylvania.

Allied Chemical and Dye (ACD). Incorporated December 17, 1920 in New York.

Allis-Chalmers Manufacturing Co. (AH). Incorporated March 15, 1913 in Delaware.

Alpha Portland Cement (AHP). Incorporated January 21, 1910 in New York.

Amalgamated Leather (ALR). Incorporated March 4, 1910 in Delaware.

Amerada Corporation (ARC). Incorporated February 7, 1920 in Delaware.

American Agricultural Chemical (Delaware). (AHD). Incorporated December 8, 1913 in Delaware.

American Bank Note (ABN). Incorporated February 19, 1906 in New York.

American Brake Shoe (ABK). Incorporated October 10, 1910 in Delaware.

American Can (AC). Incorporated March 19, 1901 in New Jersey.

American Car and Foundry (AF). Incorporated February 20, 1899 in New Jersey.

American Chicle (ACJ). Incorporated June 2, 1899 in New Jersey.

American Colortype (AOY). Incorporated February 21, 1902 in New Jersey.

American Commercial Alcohol (ACF). Incorporated April 19, 1928 in Maryland.

American Crystal Sugar (ABS). Incorporated March 24, 1899 in New Jersey.

American Encaustic Tiling (AEN). Incorporated February 24, 1936 in New York.

American European (AMU). Incorporated October 19, 1925 in Delaware.

American Express (AMX). Organized November 25, 1868 under New York Laws—not incorporated.

American and Foreign Power (AFW). Incorporated December 19, 1923 in Maine.

American Hawaiian Steamship Co. (AHS). Incorporated May 18, 1899 in New Jersey.

American Hide and Leather (HI). Incorporated May 3, 1899 in New Jersey.

American Home Products (HPT). Incorporated February 4, 1926 in Delaware.

American Ice (IS). Incorporated March 11, 1889 in New Jersey

American International (AL). Incorporated November 23, 1915 in New York.

American Locomotive (ALO). Incorporated June 10, 1901 in New York.

American Machinery and Foundry (AFX). Incorporated March 26, 1900 in New Jersey.

American Machinery and Metals (AME). Incorporated March 27, 1930 in Delaware.

American Metal (AMM). Incorporated June 17, 1887 in New York.

American News (New York Corporation) (ANC). Incorporated May 24, 1918 in New York.

American Power and Light (AOW). Incorporated September 20, 1909 in Maine.

American Radiator and Standard Sanitary Co. (ADT). Incorporated March 26, 1929 in Delaware.

American Rolling Mill (AGM). Incorporated June 29, 1917 in Ohio.

American Safety Razor (ARZ). Incorporated July 22, 1919 in Virginia.

American Seating (AMZ). Incorporated June 21, 1926 in New Jersey.

American Shipbuilding (ASU). Incorporated March 16, 1899 in New Jersey.

American Smelting and Refining (AR). Incorporated April 4, 1899 in New Jersey.

American Snuff Co. (SNU). Incorporated March 12, 1900 in New Jersey.

American Steel Foundries (FJ). Incorporated June 26, 1902 in New Jersey.

American Stores (ASC). Incorporated March 29, 1917 in Delaware.

American Sugar Refining (ASR). Incorporated January 10, 1891 in New Jersey.

American Sumatra Tobacco (AMS). Incorporated February 12, 1910 in Georgia.

American Telephone and Telegraph Co. (T). Incorporated March 3, 1885 in New York.

American Water Works and Electric Co. (AWW). Incorporated June 16, 1927 in Delaware.

American Woolen (WY). Incorporated March 29, 1899 in New Jersey. However, in this case records indicate that this stock was reincorporated on February 15, 1916 in Massachusetts.

American Zinc Lead and Smelting (ZA). Incorporated January 26, 1899 in Maine.

Anaconda Copper Mining Co. (C). Incorporated June 18, 1895 in Montana.

Anaconda Wire and Copper (AWC). Incorporated February 20, 1929 in Delaware.

Anchor Cap Corporation (ARH). Incorporated September 13, 1928 in Delaware.

Andes Copper Mining Co. (ADE). Incorporated January 20, 1916 in Delaware.

A.P.W. Paper (ABP). Incorporated July 19, 1877 in New York.

Archer-Daniels-Midland Co. (ADD). Incorporated May 2, 1923 in Delaware.

Armour-(Delaware) PFD. (AMD). Incorporated December 27, 1922 in Delaware.

Armour and Co. (AM). Incorporated April 7, 1900 in Illinois.

Armstrong Corp (ACK). Incorporated December 30, 1891 in Pennsylvania.

Arnold Constable (ACT). Incorporated September 19, 1925 in Delaware.

Artloom Corporation (ARR). Incorporated February 24, 1925 in Pennsylvania.

Associated Dry Goods (DG). Incorporated May 24, 1916 in Virginia.

Atchison, Topeka and Santa Fe Ry. (A). Incorporated December 12, 1895 in Kansas.

Atlantic Coast Line R.R. (AX). Incorporated March 14, 1836 in Virginia. Name to present title April 23, 1900.

Atlantic Gulf and West Indies Steamship Co. (AG). Incorporated November 25, 1908 in Maine.

Atlantic Refining (AFI). Incorporated April 29, 1870 in Pennsylvania.

Atlas Powder Co. (APW). Incorporated October 18, 1912 in Delaware.

Stocks Listed on The New York Stock Exchange

Atlas Tack Corporation (AKO). Incorporated January 30, 1920 in New York.

Auburn Automobile (AAC). Incorporated June 25, 1919 in Indiana.

Austin Nichols and Co. (ANO). Incorporated August 23, 1919 in Virginia.

Aviation Corporation of Delaware (AVC). Incorporated March 1, 1929 in Delaware.

Baldwin Locomotive Works (B). Incorporated June 7, 1911 in Pennsylvania. Sun 15 degrees Gemini; Moon 27 degrees Libra; Neptune 19 degrees Cancer; Uranus 28 degrees Capricorn Retrograde; Saturn 14 degrees Taurus; Jupiter 5 degrees Scorpio Retrograde; Mars 3 degrees Aries; Venus 28 degrees Cancer; Mercury 22 degrees Taurus; the Moon's North Node 8 degrees Taurus.

Bangor and Aroostook R.R. (BNK). Incorporated February 13, 1891 in Maine.

Barber Asphalt Co., Inc. (AS). Incorporated May 19, 1903 in New Jersey.

Barker Brothers (BKR). Incorporated March 15, 1928 in Maryland.

Barnsdall Oil Co. (BDL). Incorporated November 13, 1916 in Delaware.

Bayuk Cigar (BY). Incorporated May 21, 1920 in Maryland.

Beatrice Creamery (BR). Incorporated November 20, 1924 in Delaware.

Beech Creek R.R. (BCH). Incorporated May 11, 1898 in Pennsylvania.

Beech-nut Packing (BNU). Incorporated December 29, 1899 in New York.

Belding Hemingway (BV). Incorporated March 2, 1926 in Connecticut.

Belgian N. RY. (BLW). Incorporated July 23, 1926 under Belgian laws.

Bendix Aviation (BEX). Incorporated April 13, 1929 in Delaware.
Beneficial Industrial Loan (BNL). Incorporated December 7, 1936 in Delaware.
Best and Co. (BST). Incorporated July 29, 1924 in New York.
Bethlehem Steel (BS). Incorporated December 10, 1904 in New Jersey.
Bigelow Sanford (BGS). Incorporated July 30, 1904 in Massachusetts.
Blaw Knox Co. (BKX). Incorporated March 12, 1906 in New Jersey.
Bloomingdale Bros. (BBL). Incorporated August 2, 1917 in New York.
Blumenthal Co. (SBM). Incorporated June 30, 1899 in New York.
Black and Decker (BDK). Incorporated September 10, 1910 in Maryland.
Boeing Airplane Co. (BOE). Incorporated July 19, 1934 in Delaware.
Bohn Aluminum and Brass (BHL). Incorporated October 24, 1924 in Michigan.
Bond Stores, Inc. (BND). Incorporated March 13, 1937 in Maryland.
Borden Company (BDO). Incorporated April 24, 1899 in New Jersey.
Borg Warner Corporation (BOR). Incorporated May 9, 1928 in Illinois.
Bower Roller Bearing Co. (BRB). Incorporated June 23, 1910 in Michigan.
Bridgeport Brass (BRI). Incorporated April 7, 1882 in Connecticut.
Briggs Manufacturing (BGJ). Incorporated November 29, 1909 in Michigan.
Briggs and Stratton (BGG). Incorporated July 1, 1924 in Delaware.

Bristol Myers (BM). Incorporated August 11, 1933 in Delaware.

Brooklyn and Queens Transit Co. (BQT). Incorporated July 1, 1929 in New York.

Brooklyn Manhattan Transit Co. (BMT). Incorporated May 24, 1923 in New York.

Brooklyn Union Gas (BU). Incorporated September 7, 1895 in New York.

Brown Shoe Co. (BW). Incorporated January 2, 1913 in New York.

Brunswick, Balke-Collender (BCC). Incorporated December 31, 1907 in Delaware.

Bucyrus Erie (BEY). Incorporated November 3, 1927 in Delaware.

Budd Manufacturing Co. (BDM). International Corporation. Incorporated August 7, 1930 in Delaware.

Budd Wheel Co. (BWC). Incorporated June 29, 1921 in Pennsylvania.

Bullard Co. (BUD). Incorporated September 6, 1894 in Connecticut

Burlington Mills Corporation (BUR). Incorporated February 15, 1937 in Delaware.

Burroughs Adding Machine (BGH). Incorporated January 16, 1905 in Michigan.

Bush Terminal Co. (BH). Incorporated February 10, 1902 in New York.

Bush Terminal Building (BHB). Incorporated January 31, 1905 in New York.

Butler Bros. (BBR). Incorporated June 7, 1887 in Illinois.

Butte Copper and Zinc (BC). Incorporated November 22, 1904 in Maine.

A.M. Byers (ABY). Incorporated July 9, 1903 in Pennsylvania.

Byran Jackson Co. (BJC). Incorporated November 25, 1927 in Delaware.

California Packing Co. (CFF). Incorporated October 19, 1916 in New York.

Callahan Zinc-lead (CIM). Incorporated June 12, 1912 in Arizona.

Calumet and Hecla (CAH). Incorporated September 1, 1923 in Michigan.

Campbell Wyant and C Foundry (CWT). Incorporated November 28, 1927 in Michigan.

Canada Dry Ginger Ale (DGL). Incorporated June 1, 1925 in Delaware.

Canada Southern Railway (CSA). Incorporated February 28, 1868 in Canada.

Canadian Pacific Railway (CP). Incorporated February 16, 1881 in Canada.

Cannon Mills (CAM). Incorporated July 6, 1928 in North Carolina.

Capital Administration "A" (CAD). Incorporated October 18, 1928 in Maryland.

Carolina C and O Railway (CCL). Incorporated January 26, 1905 in Virginia.

Carpenter Steel (CRS). Incorporated November 4, 1904 in New Jersey.

Case (JI) Company (CTM). Incorporated February 21, 1880 in Wisconsin.

Caterpillar Tractor (CTR). Incorporated April 15, 1925 in California.

Celanese Corporation (CLZ). Incorporated January 5, 1918 in Delaware.

Celotex Corporation (CLO). Incorporated July 16, 1930 in Delaware.

Central Aguirre Association (CEG). Incorporated August 1, 1928 in Massachusetts.

Central Foundry (CFD). Incorporated March 1, 1901 in New Jersey.

Stocks Listed on The New York Stock Exchanges

Central Violeta Sugar. Incorporated September 5, 1936 in Cuba.

Century Ribbon (CTY). Incorporated December 16, 1922 in New York.

Cerro De Pasco Copper Corporation (CDP). Incorporated October 26, 1915 in New York.

Certain-teed Products (CRT). Incorporated January 30, 1917 in Maryland.

Champion Paper and Fibre (CMP). Incorporated November 3, 1893 in Ohio.

Checker Cab Manufacturing Co. (CHC). Incorporated February 19, 1923 in New Jersey.

Chesapeake and Ohio Railway Co. (CO). Incorporated July 1, 1878 in Virginia.

Chesapeake Corporation (CHK). Incorporated May 7, 1927 in Maryland.

Chicago and Eastern Illinois (CE). Incorporated December 13, 1920 in Illinois.

Chicago and Northwestern Railway Co. (NW). Incorporated June 7, 1859 in Illinois.

Chicago Great Western Railroad Co. (GW). Incorporated August 11, 1909 in Illinois.

Chicago Mail Order (CML). Incorporated December 15, 1902 in Illinois.

Chicago, Milwaukee, St. Paul and Pacific R.R. Co. (ST). Incorporated March 31, 1927 in Wisconsin.

Chicago Pneumatic Tool (CGG). Incorporated December 28, 1901 in New Jersey.

Chicago, Rock Island and Pacific Railway (RI). Incorporated June 2, 1880 in Illinois.

Chicago Yellow Cab (TXY). Incorporated October 27, 1916 in New York.

Chickasha Cotton Oil (CIK). Incorporated November 17, 1919 in Delaware.

Childs Company (CDI). Incorporated December 6, 1923 in New York.
Chile Copper (CHL). Incorporated April 16, 1913 in Delaware.
Chrysler Corporation (K). Incorporated June 6, 1925 in Delaware.
Cincinnati, Sandusky and Cleveland (CSC). Incorporated January 11, 1868 in Ohio.
City Ice and Fuel (CFY). Incorporated July 17, 1894 in Ohio.
City Investing Co. (CNV). Incorporated December 2, 1904 in New York.
City Stores (CSS). Incorporated November 5, 1923 in Delaware.
Clark Equipment (CLQ). Incorporated December 27, 1916 in Michigan.
Cleveland Graph Bronze (CLE). Incorporated March 22, 1919 in Ohio.
Cleveland and Pittsburg. Incorporated April 18, 1853 in Pennsylvania.
Cluett Peabody (CLU). Incorporated February 4, 1913 in New York.
Coca Cola Co. (KO). Incorporated September 5, 1919 in Delaware.
Coca Cola International (KOC). Incorporated November 18, 1922 in Delaware.
Colgate-Palmolive-Peet (CPL). Incorporated July 25, 1923 in Delaware.
Collins and Aikman Corporation (CK). Incorporated July 8, 1927 in Delaware.
Colonial Beacon Oil (CBD). Incorporated May 20, 1919 in Massachusetts.
Colorado Fuel and Iron Co. (CF). Incorporated October 21, 1892 in Colorado.
Columbia and Southern Railway (CX). Incorporated July 28, 1909 in Maine.
Columbia Broadcasting System (CBS). Incorporated January 27, 1927 in New York.

Columbia Gas and Electric Corporation (AG). Incorporated September 30, 1926 in Delaware.

Columbia Carbon (CBN). Incorporated August 24, 1921 in Delaware.

Columbia Pictures (CPS). Incorporated January 10, 1924 in New York.

Commercial Credit (CMO). Incorporated May 31, 1912 in Delaware.

Commercial Investment Trust Corporation (CW). January 28, 1924 in Delaware.

Commercial Solvents Corporation (CV). Incorporated December 13, 1919 in Maryland.

Commonwealth and Southern Corporation (CW). Incorporated May 23, 1929 in Delaware.

Commonwealth Edison (CWE). Incorporated October 17, 1913 in Delaware.

Conde Nast Publishing Co. (CDD). Incorporated December 13, 1922 in New York.

Congoleum-Nairn, Incorporated (COG). Incorporated June 21, 1919 in New York.

Congress Cigar (CNG). Incorporated January 14, 1926 in Delaware.

Conn Railway and Lighting (CRW). Incorporated July 2, 1895 in Connecticut.

Consolidated Cigar (CGR). Incorporated May 14, 1919 in Delaware.

Consolidated Edison (ED). Incorporated November 10, 1884 in New York.

Consolidated Film Industry (CFM). Incorporated January 7, 1928 in Delaware.

Consolidated Gas and Electric Co. New York (G). Incorporated November 10, 1884 in New York.

Consolidated Laundries (LAU). Incorporated December 8, 1925 in Maryland.

Consolidated Oil Corporation (CNI). Incorporated September 9, 1919 in New York.

Consolidated Railroad Cuba (CCU). Incorporated July 28, 1924 under Cuban laws.

Consolidated Textile Corporation (CTX). Incorporated September 27, 1919 in Delaware.

Container Corporation (CNR). Incorporated June 18, 1926 in Delaware.

Continental Baking Corporation (CI). Incorporated November 6, 1924 in Maryland.

Continental Can Co., Incorporated (CH). Incorporated January 17, 1913 in New York.

Continental Diamond Fibre (CDH). Incorporated January 28, 1929 in Delaware.

Continental Insurance (CIS). Incorporated January 7, 1853 in New York.

Continental Motor (CMR). Incorporated January 2, 1917 in Virginia.

Continental Oil Co. (CLL). Incorporated October 8, 1920 in Delaware.

Continental Steel (CT). Incorporated June 21, 1927 in Indiana.

Corn Exchange Bank. Incorporated August 28, 1858 in Pennsylvania.

Corn Products (CFG). Incorporated February 6, 1906 in New Jersey.

Coty Incorporated (COT). Incorporated December 22, 1922 in Delaware.

Crane Company (CCO). Old Company established in 1855 in Illinois. Name changed to present title January 23, 1932.

Cream of Wheat (CWH). Incorporated March 18, 1929 in Delaware.

Crosley Radio (CR). Incorporated June 30, 1919 in Ohio.

Crown Cork and Seal Company, Incorporated (CCK). Incorporated December 19, 1927 in New York.

Crown Zellerbach (CEZ). Incorporated January 6, 1926 in Delaware.

Crucible Steel (XA). Incorporated July 21, 1900 in New York.

Cuba Company (CUB). Incorporated April 25, 1900 in New York.

Cuba Railroad Company (CBR). Incorporated March 6, 1907 in Cuba.

Cuban American Sugar (CSU). Incorporated September 19, 1906 in New Jersey.

Cudahy Packing (CUX). Incorporated October 7, 1915 in Maine.

Curtis Publishing Company (CPC). Incorporated July 6, 1914 in Pennsylvania.

Curtis Wright Corporation (CWZ). Incorporated August 9, 1929 in Delaware.

Cushman's Sons (CHS). Incorporated November 25, 1914 in New York.

Cutler Hammer, Incorporated (CEH). Incorporated December 7, 1928 in Delaware.

Davega Stores Corporation (DVG) Incorporated June 12, 1928 in Delaware.

Davison Chemical Corporation (DRC). Incorporated October 30, 1935 in Maryland.

Deere and Company (DER). Organized March 8, 1911 in Illinois.

Deisel-Wemer-Gilbert (DW). Incorporated January 23, 1929 in Ohio.

Delaware and Hudson (DH). Incorporated December 1, 1928 in New York.

Delaware, Lackawanna and Western Railroad Company (DL). Old company established April 7, 1832. Name changed to present title April 14, 1851 in Delaware.

Denver and Rio Grande Western Railroad Company (DGR). Incorporated November 15, 1920 in Delaware.

Detroit Edison (DTE). Incorporated January 17, 1903 in New York.

Detroit and Mackinac (DET). Incorporated December 29, 1894 in Michigan.
Devoe and Raynolds (DRS). Incorporated April 6, 1917 in New York.
Diamond Match (DN). Incorporated February 14, 1930 in Delaware.
Diamond T Motor (DTM). Incorporated November 22, 1915 in Indiana.
Distillers C.P. Seagrams (DCS). Incorporated March 2, 1928 in Canada.
Dixie Vortex (DV). Incorporated August 8, 1929 in Delaware.
Dome Mines, Ltd. (D). Incorporated July 7, 1923 in Canada.
Dominion Stores, Ltd. (DOS). Incorporated October 3, 1919 in Canada.
Douglas Aircraft Company, Incorporated (DOU). Incorporated November 30, 1928 in Delaware.
Dow Chemical (DOW). Incorporated May 18, 1897 in Michigan.
Dresser Manufacturing (DMY). Incorporated December 13, 1905 in Pennsylvania.
Duluth South Shore and Atlantic Railway (DS). Incorporated March 9, 1887 in Michigan.
Dunhill International (DHI). Incorporated October 27, 1923 in Delaware.
Duplan Silk Corporation (DPS). Incorporated April 16, 1917 in Delaware.
Dupont de Nemours (DD). Incorporated September 14, 1915 in Delaware.
Duquesne Light (DQU). Incorporated August 5, 1903 in Pennsylvania.
Eastern Rolling Mill (ER). Incorporated June 26, 1919 in Maryland.
Eastman Kodak (EK). Incorporated October 24, 1901 in New Jersey.

Eaton Manufacturing Company (ENX). Incorporated August 28, 1916 in Ohio.

Electric Storage Battery (EG). Incorporated June 5, 1888 in New Jersey.

Elk Horn Coal (EH). Incorporated February 23, 1937 in West Virginia.

Endicott Johnson (EJ). Incorporated April 1, 1919 in New York.

Engineers Public Service (EPU). Incorporated June 23, 1925 in Delaware.

Eitingon Schild Company (EGS). Incorporated June 30, 1914 in New York.

Electric & Musical Industries (EMI). Incorporated April 20, 1931 in England.

Electric Auto-lite Company (ELO). Incorporated May 31, 1922 in Ohio.

Electric Boat (ELB). Incorporated May 29, 1923 in New Jersey.

Electric Power and Light (EL). Incorporated March 11, 1925 in Maine.

Equitable Office Building (EQ). Incorporated April 23, 1913 in New York.

Erie Railroad Company (E). Incorporated November 14, 1895 in New York.

Erie and Pittsburgh Railroad (EP). Incorporated April 1, 1838 in Pennsylvania.

Eureka Vacuum Cleaner (EU). Incorporated August 20, 1910 in Michigan.

Evans Products (EV). Incorporated December 26,1923 in Delaware.

Ex-Cell-O (EXL). Incorporated July 9, 1919 in Michigan.

Exchange Buffet (EXY). Incorporated July 26, 1913 in New York.

Fairbanks Company (VI). Incorporated June 11, 1891 in New Jersey.

Fairbanks Morse and Company (FKM). Incorporated June 30, 1891 in Illinois.

Federal Light and Traction (FDT). Incorporated April 13, 1910 in New York.

Federal Mining and Smelting (FS). Incorporated June 25, 1903 in Delaware.

Federal Motor Truck Company (FMT). Incorporated February 14, 1910 in Michigan.

Federal Screw Works (FRW). Incorporated June 23, 1919 in Michigan.

Federal Water Service Corporation (FWS). Incorporated June 21, 1926 in Delaware.

Federated Department Stores (FDS). Incorporated November 25, 1929 in Delaware.

Fidelity-Phenix Fire Insurance Company (FPX). Incorporated September 10, 1853 in New York.

Filene's (Wm). Sons (FFL). Incorporated August 19, 1912 in Massachusetts.

Firestone Tire and Rubber Company (FIR). Incorporated March 4, 1910 in Ohio.

First National Stores, Incorporated (FST). Incorporated August 25, 1917 in Massachusetts.

Flintkote (FIK). Incorporated July 12, 1917 in Massachusetts.

Florence Stove (FLS). Incorporated March 26, 1914 in Massachusetts.

Florsheim Shoe (FLO). Incorporated December 22, 1922 in Illinois.

Follansbee Bros. (FLZ). Incorporated September 6, 1894 in Pennsylvania.

Food Machinery (FDM). Incorporated August 10, 1928 in Delaware.

Foster Wheeler Corporation (FWC). Incorporated February 1, 1910 in New York.

Stocks Listed on The New York Stock Exchange

Francisco Sugar (FRA). Incorporated February 20, 1899 in New Jersey.

Franklin Simon (FIS). Incorporated September 13, 1924 in New York.

Freeport Sulphur (FT). Incorporated September 30, 1930 in Delaware.

Gabriel Company (GRR). Incorporated April 25, 1925 in Ohio.

Gair (Robt) Incorporated (GAI). Incorporated April 6, 1932 in Delaware.

Gamewell Company (GAC). Incorporated May 24, 1924 in Massachusetts.

Gar Wood Industries (GAR). Incorporated January 28, 1922 in Michigan.

Gaylord Containers Corporation (GC). Incorporated June 16, 1937 in Maryland.

General American Investment (GAM). Incorporated October 15, 1928 in Delaware.

General American Transportation (GMT). Incorporated July 5, 1916 in New York.

General Baking (GBG). Incorporated June 6, 1911 in New York.

General Bronze (GLZ). Incorporated November 21, 1927 in New York.

General Cable (GGN). Incorporated April 15, 1902 in New Jersey.

General Cigar (GY). Incorporated April 28, 1906 in New York.

General Electric Company (GL). Incorporated April 15, 1892 in New York.

General Foods Corporation (GF). Incorporated February 11, 1922 in Delaware.

General Gas and Electric (GGS). Incorporated July 21, 1925 in Delaware.

General Mills, Incorporated (GIS). Incorporated June 20, 1928 in Delaware. Sun 28 degrees Gemini; Moon 4 degrees Leo; Neptune 26 degrees Leo; Uranus 7 degrees Aries; Saturn 14 degrees

Sagittarius Retrograde; Jupiter 3 degrees Taurus; Mars 25 degrees Aries; Venus 25 degrees Gemini; Mercury 11 degrees Cancer Retrograde; Moon's North Node 8 degrees Gemini.

General Motors Corporation (GM). Incorporated October 13, 1916 in Delaware.

General Outdoor Advertising (GVZ). Incorporated February 7, 1925 in New Jersey.

General Printing Ink (GPI). Incorporated March 28, 1929 in Delaware.

General Public Service (GPV). Incorporated December 17, 1925 in Delaware.

General Railway Signal Company (GRS). Incorporated June 13, 1904 in New York.

General Realty and Utilities (GRY). Incorporated January 18, 1929 in Delaware.

General Refractories (GRX). Incorporated October 24, 1922 in Pennsylvania.

General Steel Castings Corporation (GRL). Incorporated December 11, 1928 in Delaware.

General Theatre Equity (GTE). Incorporated May 20, 1936 in Delaware.

General Time Instruments (CGLI). Incorporated November 20, 1930 in Delaware.

General Tire and Rubber (GTR). Incorporated September 14, 1915 in Ohio.

Gillette Safety Razor (GIL). Incorporated September 10, 1917 in Delaware.

Gimbel Brothers (GI). Incorporated August 22, 1922 in New York.

Glidden Company (GLN). Incorporated December 11, 1917 in Ohio.

Gobel (Adolf) Incorporated (GGO). Incorporated August 20, 1926 in New York.

Goebel Brewing Company (GBL). Incorporated November 15, 1932 in Michigan.

Gold and Stock Telegraph (GSX). Incorporated August 10, 1867 in New York.

The B.F. Goodrich Company (GG). Incorporated May 2, 1912 in New York.

Goodyear Tire and Rubber Company (GOR). Incorporated August 29, 1898 in Ohio.

Gotham Silk Hosiery Company (GHM). Incorporated October 27, 1925 in Delaware.

Graham-Paige Motors Corporation (GHR). Incorporated September 28, 1909 in Michigan.

Granby Construction Mining, Smelting and Powder Company, Ltd. (GB). Incorporated March 29, 1901 in British Columbia.

Grand Union (GUX). Inc. May 17, 1928 in Delaware.

Granite City Steel (GRC). Incorporated November 1, 1927 in Delaware.

Grant (W.T.) Company (GTY). Incorporated February 10, 1927 in Delaware.

Great Northern Iron Ore Properties (OR). Incorporated December 7, 1906 in Minnesota.

Great Northern Railway (GQ). Incorporated March 1, 1856 in Minnesota.

Great Western Sugar (GSW). Incorporated January 12, 1905 in New Jersey.

Green Bay and Western (GBW). Incorporated May 27, 1896 in Wisconsin.

Greene Cananea Copper (GNP). Incorporated December 26, 1906 in Minnesota.

Green (H.L.) (GRN). Incorporated November 17, 1932 in New York.

Greyhound Corporation (GEY). Incorporated September 20, 1926 in Delaware.

Guantananio Sugar (GS). Incorporated February 9, 1905 in New Jersey.
Gulf, Mobile and Northern (GU). Incorporated December 18, 1916 in Alabama.
Hackensack Water (HWA). Incorporated April 25, 1893 in New Jersey.
Hall (W.F.) Printing (HPG). Incorporated January 25, 1893 in Illinois.
Hamilton Watch (HMW). Incorporated December 14, 1892 in Pennsylvania.
Hanna (M.A.) (HNA). Incorporated December 9, 1922 in Ohio.
Harb-Walker (HKM). Incorporated June 30, 1902 in Pennsylvania.
Hat Corporation (HAT). Incorporated April 29, 1932 in Delaware.
Hayes Body Corporation (HYB). Incorporated May 9, 1910 in Michigan.
Hazel Atlas Glass (HZT). Incorporated October 3, 1901 in West Virginia.
Hecker Products (HP). Incorporated December 20, 1928 in New Jersey.
Helme (G.W.) Company (GH). Incorporated December 2, 1911 in New Jersey.
Hercules Motor Corporation (HMO). Incorporated June 8, 1923 in Ohio.
Hercules Powder Company (HPC). Incorporated October 17, 1912 in Delaware.
Hershey Chocolate Corporation (HSY). Incorporated October 24, 1927 in Delaware.
Hinde and Dau Paper Company (HDP). Incorporated March 4, 1900 in West Virginia.
Holland Furnace Company (HLN). Reincorporated August 29, 1934 in Michigan.
Hollander, (A.) And Son (HLL). Incorporated June 27, 1919 in Delaware.
Holly Sugar (HLY). Incorporated April 4. 1916 in New York.

Homestake Mining Company (HM). Incorporated November 5, 1877 in California.

Houdaille-Hershey Corporation (HH). Incorporated January 30, 1929 in Michigan.

Household Finance Corporation (HOF). Incorporated July 21, 1925 in Delaware.

Houston Oil Company of Texas (HO). Incorporated July 5, 1901 in Texas.

Howe Sound (HW). Incorporated August 22, 1903 in Maine.

Hudson and Manhattan (HX). Incorporated December 1, 1906 in New York.

Hudson Bay Mining and Smelting Ltd. (HBM). Incorporated December 27, 1927 in Canada.

Hudson Motor Car (HMT). Incorporated February 24, 1909 in Michigan.

Hupp Motor Car (H). Incorporated November 24, 1915 in Virginia.

Illinois Central Railroad Company (IL). Incorporated February 10, 1851 in Illinois.

Indian Refining Company (IRR). Incorporated August 26, 1926 in Delaware.

Industrial Rayon Corporation (ILR). Incorporated July 20, 1925 in Delaware.

Ingersoll Rand Company (IR). Incorporated June 1, 1905 in New Jersey.

Inland Steel (ILN). Incorporated February 6, 1917 in Delaware.

Inspiration Consolidated Copper Company (INS). Incorporated December 18, 1911 in Maine.

Insuranshares Certificates, Incorporated (ISH). Incorporated October 14, 1929 in Maryland.

Interborough Rapid Transit Company (IRT). Incorporated May 6, 1902 in New York.

Inter Chemical Corporation (IKN). Incorporated April 30, 1937 in Ohio.

Intercontinental Rubber (IRU). Incorporated September 25, 1922 in Delaware.

Interlake Iron (IKL). Incorporated June 23, 1905 in New York.

International Agricultural Corporation (IGL). Incorporated June 14, 1909 in New York.

International Business Machines Corporation (IMN). Incorporated June 16, 1911 in New York.

International Harvester Company (HR). Incorporated September 19, 1918 in New Jersey.

International Hydro-Electric System (IPH). Incorporated March 25, 1929 in Massachusetts.

International Merchant-Marine (MAR). Incorporated June 6, 1893 in New Jersey.

International Nickel Company of Canada, Ltd. (N.) Incorporated July 25, 1916 in Canada.

International Paper and Powder Company (IP). Incorporated November 1, 1928 in Massachusetts.

International Railways of Central America (IRC). Incorporated June 8, 1904 in New Jersey.

International Salt (ILS). Incorporated August 22, 1901 in New Jersey.

International Shoe Company (ISS). Incorporated March 16, 1921 in Delaware.

International Silver (INR). Incorporated November 19, 1898 in New Jersey.

International Telephone and Telegraph Company (IT). Incorporated June 16, 1930 in Maryland.

Interstate Department Stores (ISD). Incorporated February 14, 1928 in Delaware.

Intertype Corporation (IR). Incorporated February 1, 1916 in New York.

Island Creek Coal Company (ICR). Incorporated September 30, 1910 in Maine.

Jewel Tea Company (JW). Incorporated January 14, 1916 in New York.

Johns-Manville Corporation (JMP). Incorporated December 28, 1926 in New York.

Jones and Laughlin Steel (JL). Incorporated December 19, 1922 in Pennsylvania.

Kalamazoo Stove and Furnace (KAL). Incorporated June 24, 1901 in Michigan.

Kansas City Power and Light (KLT). Incorporated July 29, 1922 in Missouri.

Kansas City Southern (KSU). Incorporated March 19, 1900 in Missouri.

Kaufman Department Stores (KKN). Incorporated January 14, 1913 in New York.

Kayser (J.) Company (JKS). Incorporated June 2, 1911 in New York.

Keith-Albee-Orpheum (KLO). January 28, 1928 in Delaware.

Kelsey-Hayes Wheel Corporation (KW). Incorporated April 25, 1929 in New York.

Kendall Company (KLL). Incorporated November 10, 1924 in Massachusetts.

Kennecott Copper Corporation (KN). Incorporated May 3, 1915 in New York.

Keystone Steel and Wire (KES) Incorporated July 20, 1907 in Illinois.

Kimberly-Clark Corporation (KMB). Incorporated June 29, 1928 in Delaware.

Kinney, G.R. (KNX). Incorporated January 17, 1917 in New York.

Kresge, S.S. (KG). Incorporated March 9, 1916 in Michigan.

Kresge Department Stores (KDS). Incorporated August 16, 1923 in Delaware.

Kress, S.H. (KS). Incorporated June 21, 1916 in New York.

Kroeger Grocery Company (KR). Incorporated April 3, 1902 in Ohio.

Laclede Gas (LG). Incorporated March 2, 1857 in Missouri.

Lambert Company (LAM). Incorporated March 15, 1926 in Delaware.

Lane Bryant (LNY). Incorporated May 28, 1920 in Delaware.

Lee Rubber and Tire Corporation (LR). Incorporated December 15, 1915 in New York.

Lehigh Portland Cement (LPT). Incorporated November 26, 1897 in Pennsylvania.

Lehigh Valley Coal Company (LEH). Incorporated May 29, 1871 in Pennsylvania.

Lehigh Valley Railroad Company (LV). Original company incorporated April 21, 1846 in Pennsylvania. New company incorporated March 1, 1923 in New Jersey.

Lehman Corporation (LEM). Incorporated September 11, 1929 in Delaware.

Lehn and Fink (LNP). Incorporated August 4, 1925 in Delaware.

Lerner Stores (LER). Incorporated February 14, 1929 in Maryland.

Libbey-Owens-Ford Glass Company (LOF). Incorporated May 18, 1916 in Ohio.

Libby, McNeil and Libby (LJ). Incorporated August 6, 1903 in Maine.

Life Savers (LV). Incorporated August 12, 1933 in Delaware.

Liggett and Myers Tobacco Company (LM). Incorporated November 24, 1911 in New Jersey.

Lily Tulip Cup (LIL). Incorporated February 4, 1929 in Delaware.

Lima Locomotive Works (LMW). Incorporated April 25, 1916 in Virginia.

Link Belt Company (LB). Incorporated November 13, 1880 in Illinois.

Liquid Carbonic Corporation (LQT). Incorporated July 23, 1926 in Delaware.

Loews Incorporated (LW). Incorporated October 18, 1919 in Delaware.

Loft Incorporated (LF). Incorporated September 24, 1919 in Delaware.

Lone Star Cement (LCM). Incorporated November 15, 1919 in Maine.

Long-Bell Lumber (LQ). Incorporated April 5, 1884 in Missouri.

Loose-Wiles Biscuit Company (LO). Incorporated May 2, 1912 in New York.

P. Lorillard Company (LOR). Incorporated November 24, 1911 in New Jersey.

Louisville and Nashville (LN). Incorporated March 5, 1850 in Kentucky.

Louisville G. and E. (LOU). Incorporated February 17, 1913 in Delaware.

Ludlum Steel Company (LMS). Incorporated March 26, 1915 in New Jersey.

MacAndrews and Forbes Company (MAF). Incorporated May 8, 1902 in New Jersey.

Mack Trucks, Incorporated (MQ). Incorporated November 8, 1916 in New York.

Macy, R.H., Company (MZ). Incorporated May 28, 1919 in New York.

Madison Square Garden Corporation (MAQ). Incorporated May 31, 1923 in New York.

Magma Copper Company (MMX). Incorporated May 7, 1910 in Maine.

Manati Sugar Co. (MNO). Incorporated April 30, 1912 in New York.

Mandel Brothers. Inc. (MB). Incorporated April 21, 1926 in Delaware.

Manhattan Railway Company (MAN.) Incorporated November 20, 1875 in New York.

Manhattan Shirt Company (MT). Incorporated January 15, 1912 in New York.

Maracaibo Oil Exploration (MAB). Incorporated September 8, 1919 in Delaware.

Marine Midland Corporation (MM). Incorporated September 23, 1929 in Delaware.

Market Street Railway Company (MRR). Incorporated October 13, 1893 in California.

Marlin-Rockwell Corporation (MR). Incorporated December 26, 1894 in Delaware.

Marshall Field and Company (MFI). Incorporated March 7, 1901 in Illinois.

Martin, G. L., Company (MGL). Incorporated December 5, 1928 in Maryland.

Martin Parry Corporation (MRT). Incorporated May 26, 1919, in Delaware.

Mathieson Alkali Works Inc. (AKL). Incorporated August 13, 1892 in Virginia.

May Department Stores (MA). Incorporated June 4, 1910 in New York.

Maytag Company (MYG). Incorporated August 15, 1925 in Delaware.

McCall Corporation (MW). Incorporated February 6, 1913 in Delaware.

McCrory Stores (MRY). Incorporated May 20, 1915 in Delaware.

McGraw Electric (MGR). Incorporated November 17, 1926 in Delaware.

McGraw-Hill Publishing Company (MCG). Incorporated December 29, 1925 in New York.

McIntyre-Porcupine Mines Ltd. (MT). Incorporated March 16, 1911 in Canada.

McKeesport Tin Plate Company (MV). Incorporated January 2, 1902 in Pennsylvania.

McKesson and Robbins Incorporated (MCK). Incorporated August 4, 1928 in Indiana.

McLellan Stores (MLL). Incorporated June 12, 1924 in Delaware.

Mead Corporation (MEA). Incorporated February 17, 1930 in Ohio.

Melville Shoe Corporation (MES). Incorporated May 1, 1914 in New York.

Mengel Company (MGX). Incorporated July 12, 1899 in New Jersey

Mesta Machinery Company (MCC). Incorporated November 21, 1898 in Pennsylvania.

Miami Copper Company (MMP). Incorporated November 30, 1907 in Delaware.

Mid-Continent Petroleum Corporation (MPZ). Incorporated July 9, 1917 in Delaware.

Midland Steel Products Company (MPO). Incorporated March 21, 1923 in Ohio.

Milwaukee Electric Railway (MY). Incorporated January 30, 1896 in Wisconsin.

Minnesota-Honeywell (MHW). Incorporated October 27, 1927 in Delaware.

Minnesota-Moline (MMW). Incorporated March 30, 1929 in Delaware.

Minnesota Saint Paul Sault St. Marie (MSM). Incorporated June 11, 1888 in Minnesota.

Mission Corporation (MCO). Incorporated December 31, 1934 in Nevada.

Missouri-Kansas-Texas R.R. Company (KT). Incorporated July 6, 1922 in Missouri.

Missouri-Pacific R.R. Company (MOP). Incorporated March 5, 1917 in Missouri.

Mohawk Carpet Mills (MOK). Incorporated August 18, 1920 in New York.

Monsanto Chemical (MTC). Reincorporated March 28, 1933 in Delaware.

Montgomery Ward and Company (M). Incorporated December 3, 1919 in Illinois.

Morrell (John) and Company (MOL). Organized December 7, 1915 in Maine.

Morris and Essex R.R. Company (ME). Incorporated January 29, 1835 in New Jersey; road opened January 1, 1854.

Mother Lode Coalition (MOR). Incorporated April 17, 1919, in Delaware.

Motor Products Corporation (MPS). Incorporated January 28, 1926 in New York.

Motor Wheel Corporation (MRW). Incorporated January 17, 1920 in Michigan.

Mueller Brass (MUB). Incorporated December 31, 1917 in Michigan.

Mullins Manufacturing Corp (MNS). Incorporated July 19, 1919, in New York.

Munsingwear Inc. (MUN). Incorporated May 8, 1923 in Delaware.

Murphy (G.C.) Company (MPH). Incorporated December 31, 1919 in Pennsylvania.

Murray Corporation of America (MUY). Incorporated December 27, 1926 in Delaware.

Myers (P.E.) and Brothers (MBC). Incorporated November 19, 1927 in Ohio.

Nash-Kelvinator (NSK). Incorporated December 23, 1936 in Maryland.

Nashville, Chattanooga and St. Louis R.R. Co. (CHA). Incorporated January 21, 1850 in Tennessee.

National Acme (NCM). Incorporated November 17, 1916 in Ohio.

National Aviation (NLV). Incorporated June 23, 1928 in New York.

National Biscuit Company (BI). Incorporated February 3, 1898 in New Jersey.

National Bond and Investment Company (NBI). Incorporated May 27, 1921 in Delaware.

National Bond and Shares (NBS). Incorporated February 21, 1929 in Delaware.

National Cash Register Company (NCR). Incorporated January 2, 1926 in Maryland.

National Dairy Products Corp. (NPT). Incorporated December 8, 1923 in Delaware.

National Department Stores (NX). Incorporated December 22, 1922 in Delaware.

National Distillers Products Corporation (NAD). Incorporated April 18, 1924 in Virginia.

National Enameling and Stamping Company (EGK). Incorporated January 21, 1899 in New Jersey.

National Gypsum Company (NGY). Incorporated August 29, 1925 in Delaware.

National Lead Company (LT). Incorporated December 7, 1891 in New Jersey.

National Malleable and Steel Casings (NML). Incorporated December 1, 1923 in Ohio.

National Power and Light (NPL). Incorporated December 7, 1925 in New Jersey.

National Railway of Mexico (MX). Incorporated February 24, 1902 in Utah.

National Steel Corporation (NAX). Incorporated November 7, 1929 in Delaware.

National Supply of Delaware (NSC). Incorporated December 11, 1922 in Delaware.

National Tea Company (NTY). Incorporated February 6, 1903 in Illinois.

Natomas Company (NOM). Incorporated November 13, 1928 in California.

Neisner Brothers (NEB). Incorporated April 6, 1916 in New York.

Newberry, J. J. company (NE). Incorporated February 15, 1923 in Delaware.

New Orleans, Texas, and Mexico (NOX). Incorporated February 29, 1916 in Louisiana.

Newport Industries (NEP). Incorporated September 5, 1931 in Delaware.

New York Air Brake (AB). Incorporated July 1, 1890 in New Jersey.

New York Central R.R. Company (CN). Incorporated December 22, 1914 in New York.

New York, Chicago, and St. Louis (NKP). Incorporated April 11, 1923 in Ohio.

New York City Omnibus (NYB). Incorporated January 22, 1925 in New York.

New York Dock (DK). Incorporated July 18, 1901 in New York.

New York and Harlem (HAR). Incorporated April 25, 1831 in New York. Road opened May 10, 1852.

New York Investors (NYK). Incorporated January 19, 1929 in New York.

New York, Lackawanna, and Western (NL). Incorporated August 24, 1880 in New York.

New York, New Haven, and Hartford Railroad (V). Incorporated August 6, 1872 in Connecticut.

New York, Ontario and Western (OW). Incorporated January 21, 1880 in New York.

New York Shipbuilding (NSB). Incorporated November 29, 1916 in New York.

New York Steamer (NSM). Incorporated July 14, 1921 in New York.

Norfolk and Western Railway Company (NFK). Incorporated January 15, 1896 in Virginia.

Norfolk Southern (NS). Incorporated May 2, 1910 in Virginia.

North American Aviation, Inc. (NAV). Incorporated December 6, 1928 in Delaware.

North American Company (NA). Incorporated June 14, 1890 in New Jersey.

North American Edison (NAE). Incorporated March 25, 1922 in Delaware.

Northern Central Railroad Company (NNX). Incorporated December 16, 1854 in Pennsylvania.

Northern Pacific Railroad Company (NP.). Incorporated March 15, 1870 in Wisconsin.

Northern States Power. Incorporated December 23, 1909 in Delaware.

Northwestern Telegraph (NWT). Incorporated July 1, 1881 in Wisconsin.

Norwalk Tire and Rubber Company (NRT). Incorporated March 23, 1914 in Connecticut.

Ohio Oil Company (OHO). Incorporated July 30, 1887 in Ohio. Sun 6 degrees Leo; Moon 14 degrees Sagittarius; Neptune 29 degrees Taurus; Uranus 9 degrees Libra; Saturn 27 degrees Cancer; Jupiter 27 degrees Libra; Mars 12 degrees Cancer; Venus 21 degrees Virgo; Mercury 4 degrees Leo Retrograde; Moon's North Node 19 degrees Leo.

Oliver Farm Equipment (OF). Incorporated February 13, 1929 in Delaware.

Omnibus Corporation (BUZ). Incorporated April 17, 1923 in Delaware.

Oppenheim Collins (OPS). Incorporated September 10, 1924 in Delaware.

Otis Elevator Company (OT). Incorporated November 28, 1898 in New Jersey.

Outlet Company (OTU). Inc. July 18, 1925 in Rhode Island.

Outboard Marine and Manufacturing Company (OMN). Incorporated September 30, 1936 in Delaware.

Owens-Illinois Glass Company (OB). Incorporated December 16, 1907 in Ohio.

Pacific American Fishery (PCF). Incorporated May 2, 1928 in Delaware.

Pacific Coast Company (PCX). Incorporated November 29, 1897 in New Jersey.

Pacific Finance Corporation of California (PF). Incorporated February 26, 1931 in Delaware.

Pacific Gas and Electric (PCG). Incorporated October 10, 1905 in California.

Pacific Lighting Corporation (PLI). Incorporated March 21, 1907 in California.

Pacific Mills (PFS). Incorporated November 14, 1914 in British Columbia.

Pacific Telephone and Telegraph (PAC). Incorporated December 31, 1906 in California.

Pacific Western Oil (PWO). Incorporated November 10, 1928 in Delaware.

Packard Motor Car Company (PAK). Incorporated September 1, 1909 in Michigan.

Pan-American Petroleum (PP). Incorporated February 4, 1916 in Delaware.

Panhandle Products and Ref. (PDF). Incorporated October 16, 1919 in Delaware.

Paraffine Company (PAF). Incorporated November 20, 1917 in Delaware.

Paramount Pictures (PX). Incorporated July 19, 1916 in New York.

Park and Tilford (PKT). Incorporated August 6, 1923 in Delaware.

Park-Utah Consolidation Mining (PUC). Incorporated January 21, 1917 in Delaware.

Parke-Davis Company (PDC). Incorporated January 14, 1875 in Michigan.

Parker Rust-Proof Company (PRK). Incorporated May 13, 1929 in Michigan.

Parmelee Transport Company (PTE). Incorporated April 12, 1929 in Delaware.

Pathe Film (PTH). Incorporated December 28, 1914 in New York.

Patino Mines (PAE). Inc. July 5, 1924 in Delaware.

Peerless Corporation (PSS). Incorporated November 1, 1915 in Virginia.

Penick and Ford (PFK). Incorporated February 7, 1920 in Delaware.

Penney, J.C., Company (PEJ). Incorporated December 15, 1924 in Delaware.

Pennsylvania Coal and Coke (PVX). Incorporated November 11, 1911 in Pennsylvania.

Penn-Dixie Cement (DXC). Incorporated September 16, 1926 in Delaware.

Pennsylvania Glass Sand Corporation (PGS). Incorporated July 13, 1927 in Pennsylvania.

Pennsylvania Railroad Company (PA). Incorporated April 13, 1846 in Pennsylvania. Road opened February 15, 1854 in Pennsylvania.

People's Drug Stores (PDG). Incorporated April 2, 1928 in Maryland.

Peoples' Gas Light and Coke Company (PO). Incorporated February 12, 1855 in Illinois.

Peoria and Eastern (PE). Incorporated February 21, 1890 in Illinois.

Pere Marquette Railroad (PQ). Incorporated March 12, 1917 in Michigan.

Pet Milk Company (PET). Incorporated March 31, 1925 in Delaware.

Petroleum Corporation of America (PEO). Incorporated January 16, 1929 in Delaware.

Pfeiffer Brew (PFB). Incorporated February 5, 1926 in Michigan.

Phelps-Dodge Corporation (PDO). Incorporated August 10, 1885 in New York.

Philadelphia Company (PH). Incorporated March 22, 1871 in Pennsylvania.

Philadelphia Rapid Transit (PV). Incorporated May 1, 1902 in Pennsylvania.

Philadelphia Reading Coal and Iron Corporation (PRC). Incorporated December 19, 1923 in Delaware.

Philip Morris, Ltd. (MOS). Incorporated February 21, 1919 in Virginia.

Phillips Jones Corporation (PJ). Incorporated August 15, 1919 in New York.

Phillips Petroleum (P). Incorporated June 13, 1917 in Delaware.

Phoenix Hosiery Company (PXY). Incorporated November 27, 1922 in Wisconsin.

Pierce Oil Corporation (POL). Incorporated June 21, 1913 in Virginia.

Pillsbury Flour Mills (PSY). Incorporated June 23, 1909 in Delaware.

Pirelli Company (PRL). Incorporated November 3, 1920 in Italy.

Pittsburgh Coal Company (PC). Incorporated January 12, 1916 in Pennsylvania.

Pittsburgh Coke and Iron (PCK). Incorporated August 28, 1928 in Pennsylvania.

Pittsburgh, Fort Wayne And Chicago (FW). Incorporated February 28, 1862 in Pennsylvania.

Pittsburgh Screw and Bolt (PIT). Incorporated March 19, 1929 in Pennsylvania.

Pittsburgh Steel (PG). Incorporated November 11, 1901 in Pennsylvania.

Pittsburgh Terminal Coal (PPT). Incorporated April 28, 1902 in Pennsylvania.

Pittsburgh United (PUN). Incorporated March 18, 1891 in Pennsylvania.

Pittsburgh and West Virginia Railway (PW). Incorporated January 29, 1917 in Pennsylvania and West Virginia.

Pittston Company (PCO). Incorporated January 13, 1930 in Delaware.

Plymouth Oil (PYO). Incorporated October 19, 1923 in Delaware.

Pond Creek Pocahontas Company (PND). Incorporated February 20, 1923 in Maine.

Poor and Company (POR). Incorporated April 4, 1928 in Delaware.

Porto Rico American Tobacco (PRT). Incorporated September 22, 1899 in New Jersey.

Postal Telegraph and Cable (PST). Incorporated May 18, 1928 in Maryland.

Pressed Steel Car (PSL). Incorporated January 2, 1899 in New Jersey.

Proctor and Gamble Company (PGM). Incorporated May 5, 1905 in Ohio.

Public Service of New Jersey (PUB). Incorporated May 6, 1903 in New Jersey.

Public Service Electric and Gas (PEG). Incorporated July 25, 1924 in New Jersey.

Pullman Incorporated (PU). Incorporated June 21, 1927 in Delaware.

Pure Oil Company (PUY). Incorporated April 8, 1914 in Ohio.

Purity Bakeries (PTY). Incorporated December 1, 1924 in Delaware.

Quaker Stations Oil (QKR). Incorporated June 23, 1931 in Delaware.

Radio Corporation of America ®). Incorporated October 17, 1919 in Delaware.

Radio-Keith-Orpheum (RKO). Incorporated October 25, 1928 in Maryland.

Railroad Section, Illinois, Central Stock (RSY). Incorporated February 20, 1896 in New Jersey.

Raybestos-Manhattan (RAY). Incorporated July 5, 1929 in New Jersey.

Reading Company (RDG). Incorporated May 24, 1871 in Pennsylvania.

Rayonier Inc. (RNR). Incorporated November 1, 1937 in Delaware.

Real Silk Hosiery (RSH). Incorporated October 1, 1923 in Illinois.

Robert Reis and Company (RIS). Incorporated May 13, 1885 in New York.

Reliable Stores Corporation (RES). Incorporated May 12, 1925 in Maryland.

Reliance Manufacturing Company (RMC). Incorporated December 22, 1922 in Illinois.

Remington-Rand Inc. (RR). Incorporated January 25, 1927 in Delaware.

Rensselaer and Saratoga (RNS). Incorporated; leased May 1, 1871 in New York to Delaware Hudson.

Reo Motor Car (RY). Incorporated August 16, 1904 in Michigan.

Republic Steel Corporation (RBC). Incorporated May 3, 1899 in New Jersey.

Revere Copper and Brass (RVB). Incorporated December 1, 1928 in Maryland.

Reynolds Metals (RLM). Incorporated July 18, 1928 in Delaware.

Reynolds Spring Company (RSA). Incorporated July 2, 1919 in Delaware.

Reynolds (R.J.) Tobacco Company (REY). Incorporated April 3, 1899 in New Jersey.

Rhine-Westphalia Electric Power (RWE). Incorporated June 24, 1898 under German laws.

Richfield Oil Corporation (RIL). Incorporated November 14, 1936 in Delaware.

Ritter Dental Manufacturing Company (RDL). Incorporated June 30, 1926 in Delaware.

Roan Antelope Copper Manufacturing Company (RNO). Incorporated June 3, 1927 in Great Britain.

Ruberoid Company (RBR). Incorporated June 16, 1905 in New Jersey.

Rutland Railroad Company (RV). Consolidated December 23, 1901 in Vermont.

Safeway Stores, Inc (SAF). Incorporated March 24, 1926 in Maryland.

St. Joseph Lead Company (JO). Incorporated March 25, 1864 in New York.

St. Louis-San Francisco Railway (FN). Incorporated August 24, 1916 in Missouri.

Savage Arms (SA). Incorporated August 14, 1915 in Delaware.

Schenley Distillers (SHN). Incorporated July 11, 1933 in Delaware.

Schulte Retail Stores (SHO). Incorporated September 5, 1919 in Delaware.

Seaboard Air Line (SBD). Incorporated December 1, 1898 in North Carolina and Virginia.

Seaboard Oil of Delaware (MSX). Incorporated September 12, 1919 in Delaware.

Seagrave Corporation (SVE). Incorporated January 5, 1925 in Michigan.

Sears, Roebuck Company (S). Incorporated June 16, 1906 in New York. Sun 24 degrees Gemini; Moon 24 degrees Aries; Neptune 9 degrees Cancer; Uranus 7 degrees Capricorn Retrograde; Saturn 14 degrees Pisces; Jupiter 20 degrees Gemini; Mars 3 degrees Cancer; Venus 25 degrees Cancer; Mercury 3 degrees Cancer; Moon's North Node 14 degrees Leo.

Servel, Incorporated (SVL). Incorporated December 16, 1927 in Delaware.

Sharon Steel Corporation (SSH). Incorporated October 8, 1900 in Pennsylvania.

Sharp and Dohme (SDH). Incorporated December 27, 1926 in Maryland.

Shattuck (F.G.) Company (FHK). Incorporated May 31, 1936 in Massachusetts.

Shell Union Oil (SUX). Incorporated February 8, 1922 in Delaware.

Silver King Coalition (SKC). Incorporated May 20, 1907 in Nevada.

Simmons Company (SIM). Incorporated December 14, 1915 in Delaware.

Simms Petroleum Company (SV). Incorporated June 27, 1919 in Delaware.

Simonds Saw and Steel Company (SDS). Incorporated December 20, 1922 in Massachusetts.

Skelly Oil Company (SYE). Incorporated August 20, 1919 in Delaware.

Sloss-Sheffield Steel (SLS). Incorporated August 16, 1899 in New Jersey.

Smith (A.O.) Corporation (SMC). Incorporated November 13, 1916 in New York.

Smith (L.C.) Corona Typewriters (SLT). Incorporated October 30, 1924 in New York.

Snider Packing Corporation (SNR). Incorporated September 3, 1919 in New York.

Socony-Vacuum Oil (SOV). Incorporated August 10, 1882 in New York.

Solvay-American (SO). Incorporated January 24, 1927 in Delaware.

South America Gold and Platinum (SGP). Incorporated October 11, 1916 in Delaware.

South Porto Rico Sugar (PSU). Incorporated November 16, 1900 in New Jersey.

Southern California Edison (SCE). Incorporated July 6, 1909 in California.

Southern Dairies, Incorporated (SD). Incorporated August 5, 1925 in Delaware.

Southern Pacific Company (SX). Incorporated March 17, 1884 in Kentucky.

Southern Railway (SR). Incorporated February 20, 1894 in Virginia.

Spalding (A.G.) And Bros. (AGS). Incorporated February 2, 1892 in New Jersey.

Sparks-Withington Company (SKW). Incorporated December 24, 1919 in Ohio.

Spear and Company (SST). Incorporated December 15, 1903 in New Jersey.

Spencer Kellogg and Sons (SK). Incorporated August 13, 1912 in New York.

Sperry Corporation (SPC). Incorporated April 12, 1933 in Delaware.

Spicer Manufacturing Company (SSY). This stock was incorporated October 12, 1916 in the State of Virginia.

Spiegel, Incorporated (SMS). Incorporated April 28, 1928 in Delaware. Sun 7 degrees Taurus; Moon 27 degrees Leo; Neptune 26 degrees Leo Retrograde; Uranus 5 degrees Aries; Saturn 18 degrees Sagittarius Retrograde; Jupiter 21 degrees Aries; Mars 16 degrees Pisces; Venus 20 degrees Aries; Mercury 2 degrees Taurus; Moon's North Node 11 degrees Gemini.

Standard Brands (SB). Incorporated June 28, 1929 in Delaware.

Standard Common Tobacco (SDT). Incorporated August 10, 1916 in Delaware.

Standard Gas and Electric Company (SG). Incorporated April 28, 1910 in Delaware.

Standard Investing Corporation (SVG). Incorporated January 31, 1927 in Maryland.

Standard Oil of California (SCD). Incorporated January 27, 1926 in Delaware.

Standard Oil of Indiana (SN). Incorporated June 18, 1889 in Indiana.

Standard Oil of Kansas (SKL). Incorporated December 24, 1892 in Kansas.

Standard Oil of New Jersey (J). Incorporated August 5, 1882 in New Jersey.

Starrett, (L.S). (SCX). Incorporated February 20, 1929 in Delaware.

Sterling Products, Incorporated (STY). Incorporated April 9, 1932 in Delaware.

Stewart-Warner Corporation (STX). Incorporated December 20, 1912 in Virginia.

Stokely Bros. and Company (SBC). Incorporated August 13, 1936 in Indiana.

Stone and Webster (SW). Incorporated June 25, 1929 in Delaware.

Studebaker Corporation (STU). Incorporated January 26, 1935 in Delaware.

Sun Oil Company (SUN). Incorporated May 2, 1901 in New Jersey.

Sunshine Mining Company (SMN). Incorporated May 28, 1918 in Washington (State).

Superheater Company (SUH). Incorporated October 25, 1912 in Delaware.

Superior Oil Corporation (SI). Incorporated October 26, 1917 in Delaware.

Superior Steel (SSU). Incorporated December 21, 1916 in Virginia.

Sutherland Paper Company (SU). Incorporated April 3, 1917 in Michigan.

Sweets Company of America (SWA). Incorporated June 28, 1919 in Virginia.

Swift and Company (SWX). Incorporated April 1, 1885 in Illinois.

Swift International (SWI). (South American Company). Incorporated June 26, 1918 in Argentine Republic.

Symington-Gould (SYG). Incorporated December 2, 1924 in Maryland.

Talcott (J.) Incorporated (TLC). Incorporated December 24, 1914 in New York.

Telautograph Corporation (TZ). Incorporated November 26, 1915 in Virginia.

Tennessee Corporation (TCC). Incorporated October 11, 1916 in New York.

Texas and Pacific Railway (TP). Incorporated March 3, 1871 in Texas.

Texas Corporation (TX). Incorporated August 26, 1926 in Delaware.

Texas Gulf Products (TPX). Incorporated April 3, 1931 in Delaware.

Texas Gulf Sulphur (TG). Incorporated December 23, 1909 in Texas.

Texas Pacific Coal and Oil Company (TES). Incorporated October 4, 1888 in Texas.

Texas Pacific Land Trust (TXL). Organized February 1, 1888 in Texas.

Thatcher Manufacturing Company (TCR). Incorporated February 15, 1905 in New York.

Thermoid Company (THR). Incorporated January 28, 1929 in Delaware.

Third Avenue Railway Company (TAV). Incorporated April 10, 1910 in New York.

Thompson (J.R.) Company (THM). Incorporated April 13, 1914 in West Virginia.

Thompson Products (THO). Incorporated January 2, 1901 in Ohio.

Thompson-Starrett (TST). Incorporated December 3, 1928 in Delaware.

Tide Water Associated Oil Company (TVN). Incorporated March 5, 1926 in Delaware.

Timken-Detroit Axle Company (TDX). Incorporated June 11, 1909 in Ohio.

Timken Roller Bearing Company (TKR). Incorporated December 13, 1904 in Ohio.

Transamerica Corporation (TA). Incorporated October 11, 1928 in Delaware.

Transcontinental and Western Airline (TWA). Incorporated December 27, 1934 in Delaware.

Transue and Williams (TU). Incorporated March 3, 1930 in Delaware.

Tri-Continental Corporation (TCL). Incorporated December 31, 1929 in Maryland.

Truax-Traer Coal Company (TRC). Incorporated December 27, 1926 in Delaware.

Truscon Steel (TUX). Incorporated October 6, 1903 in Michigan.

Twenty Century Fox Film Corporation (TCF). Incorporated February 1, 1915 in New York.

Twin-City Rapid Transit Company (TWC). Incorporated June 3, 1891 in New Jersey.

Twin Coach Company (TWN). Incorporated April 5, 1927 in Delaware.

Ulen and Company (ULE). Incorporated February 10, 1922 in Delaware.

Underwood-Elliot-Fisher Company (UNX). Incorporated December 29, 1927 in Delaware.

Stocks Listed on The New York Stock Exchange

Union Bag and Paper (BP). Incorporated October 4, 1916 in New Jersey.

Union Carbide and Carbon Corporation (UN). Incorporated November 1, 1917 in New York.

Union Oil of California (UCL). Incorporated October 17, 1890 in California.

Union Pacific Railroad Company (UP). Incorporated July 1, 1897 in Utah.

Union Tank Car (UTX). Incorporated July 14, 1891 in New Jersey.

United Air Lines (ULT). Incorporated July 20, 1934 in Delaware.

United Aircraft Corporation (UAR). Incorporated July 21, 1954 in Delaware.

United American Bosch (BOS). Incorporated January 9, 1919 in New York.

United Biscuit Company (UBS). Incorporated November 3, 1927 in Delaware.

United Carbon Company (UCB). Incorporated February 19, 1925 in Delaware.

United Car Fastener Corporation (UCF). Incorporated April 12, 1928 in Massachusetts.

United Corporation (DEL.) (U). Incorporated January 7, 1929 in Delaware.

United Drug Inc. (UND). Incorporated August 14, 1933 in Delaware.

United Dyewood (UDY). Incorporated September 26, 1916 in Delaware.

United Electric Coal (UEL). Incorporated August 3, 1918 in Delaware.

United Engineer and Foundry (UEF). Consolidated on May 1, 1917 in Pennsylvania.

United Fruit (UF). Incorporated March 30, 1899 in New Jersey.

United Gas Improvement Company (UGI). Incorporated June 1, 1882 in Pennsylvania.

United Paperboard (PB). Incorporated February 29, 1912 in New Jersey.

U.S. and Foreign Securities (UFO). Incorporated October 9, 1924 in Maryland.

U.S. Distributing (UM). Incorporated June 20, 1921 in New York.

U.S. Freight Company (UFG). Incorporated 1925 in Delaware; consolidated with Central Container Company of New York January 24, 1932.

U.S. Gypsum Company (USG). Incorporated August 12, 1920 in Illinois.

U.S. Hoffman Machinery (HMY). Incorporated January 19, 1922 in Delaware.

U.S. Industrial Alcohol (UD). Incorporated October 16, 1906 in West Virginia.

U.S. Leather (LX). Incorporated June 23, 1927 in N. J.

U.S. Pipe and Foundry Company (CJ). Incorporated March 2, 1899 in New Jersey.

U.S. Realty and Improvement Company (UZ). Incorporated May 26, 1904 in New Jersey.

U.S. Rubber Company (RU). Incorporated March 30, 1892 in New Jersey.

U.S. Smelting, Refining and Mining Company (UV). Incorporated January 9, 1906 in Maine.

U.S. Steel Corporation (X). Incorporated February 23, 1901 in New Jersey. Sun 4 degrees Pisces; Moon 4 degrees Taurus; Neptune 26 degrees Gemini Retrograde; Uranus 16 degrees Sagittarius; Saturn 13 degrees Capricorn; Jupiter 6 degrees. Capricorn; Mars 2 degrees Virgo Retrograde; Venus 17 degrees Aquarius; Mercury 21 degrees Pisces; Moon's North Node 27 degrees Scorpio.

U.S. Tobacco Company (UBO). Incorporated December 2, 1911 in New Jersey.

United Stockyards (UST). Incorporated May 15, 1936 in Delaware.

United Stores (UDS). Incorporated June 8, 1929 in Delaware.

Universal Cyclop Steel Corporation (UCS). Incorporated June 22, 1908 in Pennsylvania.

Universal Leaf Tobacco (UVV). Incorporated January 25, 1918 in Virginia.

Universal Pictures (UVP). Incorporated January 10, 1925 in Delaware.

Utility Power and Light (ULA). Incorporated March 19, 1915 in Virginia.

Vadsco Sales Corporation (VAD). Incorporated August 6, 1919 in Delaware.

Van Raalte Company (VRT). Incorporated November 12, 1919, in New York.

Vanadium Corporation (VA). Incorporation September 6, 1919 in Delaware.

Vick Chemical (VIK). Incorporated August 12, 1933 in Delaware.

Vicksburg, Shreveport, and Pacific Railway (VKS). Incorporated April 23, 1901 in Louisiana.

Virginia-carolina Chemical Corporation (VC). Incorporated March 24, 1926 in Virginia.

Virginia Electric and Power (VE). Incorporated June 29, 1909 in Virginia.

Virginia Iron, Coal and Coke (VK). Incorporated January 19, 1899 in Virginia.

Virginian Railway (VA). Incorporated February 20, 1904 in Virginia.

Vulcan Detinning Company (VX). Incorporated April 26, 1902 in New Jersey.

Wabash Railway (WA). Incorporated October 22, 1915 in Indiana.

Waldorf System (WXY). Incorporated April 18, 1919 in Massachusetts.

Walgreen Company (WAG). Incorporated February 5, 1909 in Illinois.

Walker (H) G. And W. Ltd. (HIR). Incorporated December 31, 1926 in Canada.

Walworth Company (WAL). Incorporated February 12, 1872 in Massachusetts.

Ward Baking Company (WD). Incorporated December 27, 1923 in Maryland.

Warner Brothers Pictures (WB). Incorporated April 4, 1923 in Delaware.

Warren Brothers Company (WAR). Incorporated February 5, 1900 in West Virginia.

Warren Foundry and Pipe (WFP). Incorporated April 8, 1927 in Delaware.

Waukesha Motor Company (WAD). Incorporated May 28, 1906 in Wisconsin.

Webster Eisenlohr (WBS). Incorporated February 13, 1911 in Pennsylvania.

Wells Fargo and Company (WF). Incorporated February 1, 1923 in Colorado.

Wesson Oil and Snowdrift (WNO). Incorporated May 20, 1925 in Louisiana.

West Auto Supply Company (WST). Incorporated November 17, 1914 in Missouri.

Western Maryland Railway (WM). Incorporated February 15, 1917 in Maryland.

Western Pacific Railroad Corporation (WR). Incorporated June 29, 1916 in Delaware.

West Penn Electric Company (WEP). Incorporated December 11, 1925 in Maryland.

West Penn Power Company (WPP). Incorporated March 1, 1916 in Pennsylvania.

Western Union Telegraph Company (W). Incorporated April 1, 1851 in New York.

Westinghouse Air Brake (WKM). Incorporated September 28, 1869 in Pennsylvania.

Westinghouse Electric and Manufacturing Company (WX). Incorporated April 9, 1872 in Pennsylvania.

Western Electric Institute (WZ). Incorporated December 11, 1924 in New Jersey.

Westvaco Chlorine Products (WCO). Incorporated December 15, 1926 in Delaware.

Wheeling and Lake Erie (WL). Incorporated December 14, 1916 in Ohio.

Wheeling Steel (WHX). Incorporated June 21, 1920 in Delaware.

Zenith Radio Corporation (ZE). Incorporated July 5, 1923 in Illinois. Sun 12 degrees Cancer; Moon 6 degrees Aries; Neptune 16 degrees Leo; Uranus 17 degrees Pisces Retrograde; Saturn 13 degrees Libra; Jupiter 9 degrees Scorpio Retrograde; Mars 23 degrees Cancer; Venus 24 degrees Gemini; Mercury 24 degrees Gemini; Moon's North Node 14 degrees Virgo.

Zonite Products Corporation (ZP). Incorporated June 18, 1927 in Delaware. Sun 26 degrees Gemini; Moon 5 degrees Aquarius; Neptune 24 degrees Leo; Uranus 3 degrees Aries; Saturn 2 degrees Sagittarius Retrograde; Jupiter 1 degree Aries; Mars 7 degrees Leo; Venus 11 degrees Leo; Mercury 20 degrees Cancer; Moon's North Node 28 degrees Gemini.

* * *

Planetary Positions from 1850 to 1930 are given in terms of Greenwich Mean Time Noon. Planetary Positions from 1931 to 1950 are given in terms of Greenwich Mean Time Midnight.

Editor's Note: More recent information on individual stocks is available in *Planetary Stock Trading* by Bill Meridian.

Glossary

Angles: The four angular positions of a chart; that is, the first, tenth, seventh, and fourth houses. They are called the Ascendant, Midheaven, Descendant, and Nadir.

Ascendant: This is the sign and degree on the first house of a chart. It is sometimes called the "rising sign." Planets transiting this sign on the chart of the New York Stock Exchange have a powerful effect on stock market action as well as pointing out important changes in the affairs of this country.

Aspects: The angular distance between planets which determine their influence favorably or unfavorably on stock market conditions.

The square aspect is 90 degrees and exerts an unfavorable influence.

The opposition aspect is 180 degrees and exerts an unfavorable influence.

The sextile aspect is 60 degrees and exerts a favorable influence.

The trine aspect is 120 degrees and exerts a favorable influence. These four aspects are the major aspects or the most powerful aspects in strength of influence.

The minor aspects or angles of lesser influence between the planets are:

The semi-square aspect of 45 degrees which is unfavorable in influence.

Glossary

The sesquiquadrate aspect of 135 degrees which exerts an unfavorable influence.

The semi-sextile aspect of 30 degrees which exerts a favorable influence.

Conjunction: When two or more planets are placed in the same sign of the zodiac and within 9 degrees of each other they are said to be in conjunction. This is an aspect of major strength which is variable in nature and influence. The nature of the planets involved determine whether the aspect is favorable or unfavorable in influence.

Cusp: The beginning or edge of a house or section of a chart. The sign on the cusp, or line at the beginning of a house, is the ruler of that house, together with its ruling planet. Planets passing over the cusp, or line, of a house are more important than planets which have moved into this house, since the cusp is a very sensitive area.

Degree: The zodiac, which is diagramatically shown on a chart of twelve sections or houses, consists of twelve signs which contain 30 degrees each. A degree of a sign contains 60 minutes (') of longitude and each minute contains 60 seconds (") of longitude.

Descendant: The seventh cusp or house of a chart.

Ecliptic: The Sun's path as it appears to go around the Earth. In reality, it is the path of the Earth around the Sun. The ecliptic is taken as the standard line of celestial motion in our solar system. The planets move along this line sometimes to the north of the ecliptic and sometimes to the south of it. A planet's position north or south of the Sun's path determines its latitude.

Ephemeris (plural ephemerides): The ephemeris is simply an almanac of the planets' places for any certain year. It gives the geocentric longitude, declination, aspects, lunations, and other valuable information necessary in setting up a chart in this work.

Geocentric: This word is derived from two Greek words: *geo,* meaning earth, and *centric*, meaning center. It means assuming the Earth as being the center of our solar system and to study the aspects and influences of the planets as they reach the Earth. Astrology studies the planetary positions and their effects in relation to the Earth, not the Sun; therefore, in this work an ephemeris which gives the geocentric position of the planets is used. When the Sun is taken as the center of our solar system, which in reality it is, with the Earth and the other planets in relation to it, we have what is known as the heliocentric positions of the planets. *Helios* means Sun; and *centric* means center. This, however, is of no benefit to individuals on the Earth. It would be of benefit only if we lived on the Sun, since the planetary effects are taken in relation to the Sun. We want the planetary position and effects in relation to the Earth on which we live; therefore, we use the *geocentric* positions of the planets only.

House: The word "house" is used in this work to designate one-twelfth of the heavens as viewed from the Earth. These twelve segments are represented on a chart, in the shape of a wheel, and each corresponds with one of the twelve signs of the zodiac.

House Position: This is a term used to designate the number of the section of a chart in which a planet or planets fall. There are twelve houses to a chart which rotate numerically counter-clockwise.

Intercepted: Due to the shift of the horizon in relation to the birthplace, as a chart is erected north or south of the equator, a full sign of the zodiac will often fall between two cusps. The sign is then said to be "intercepted" in a house. This is most noticeable as one moves farther north or farther south of the equator. When a sign is intercepted in a house, the opposite sign is also intercepted in the opposite house. For an example of an intercepted sign, see the Chart of the New York Stock Exchange where the sign of Aries (♈) is intercepted in the tenth house, or Midheaven, of the chart, and its opposite sign of Libra (♎) is intercepted in the opposite house, which is the fourth house of the chart, sometimes called the Nadir.

Jupiter: This is the largest planet of the solar system. In this work, it represents the principle of expansion. It has a twelve-year cycle; that is, it returns to the same place in the zodiac every twelve years.

It has been found that the passage of Jupiter through the ruling sign of any country usually marks a period of prosperity for that country, particularly if it is in favorable aspect to either Uranus or Saturn at the same time. Jupiter rules the sign of Sagittarius.

Lunation: This is the name for the conjunction of the Sun and Moon which occurs every twenty-eight days in one of the twelve signs of the zodiac. The lunation during any month is often referred to as the New Moon. The method used in this book for forecasting monthly trends on th New York Stock Exchange is based on the position and aspects of the lunation each month.

Mars: This planet moves through the zodiac once every two years or on an average of about every twenty-two months. It is one of the rulers of the Midheaven of the New York Stock Exchange Chart because Aries is an intercepted sign in the tenth house of this chart, and Mars is the ruler of Aries. Aspects to this planet at the lunation are highly important because they are indicative of a coming change in the trend of stocks on the New York Stock Change. Mars represents the principle of activity and force. Active markets always have Mars aspected strongly in some manner. Study well the aspects to Mars at the lunation each month, as well as its sign position and house position in the Chart of the New York Stock Exchange. It will reveal much concerning the volume of sales for the coming month in the stock market, either as active buying or active selling of stocks.

Mercury: This planet is of minor importance in so far as this work is concerned. Its main significance is the fact that it has joint rulership over the sign of Gemini (the sign which is on the Ascendant of the chart of the United States) and the sign of Virgo, which is placed on the fourth cusp of the Chart of the New York Stock Exchange. Aspects to this planet at the monthly lunation, and the aspects which Mercury makes to the major planets, particularly Saturn and Uranus, should always be noticed. It sometimes happens that when Saturn and Uranus are in favorable or unfavorable aspect and a change in the trend of the stock market is about to occur, although neither of these planets were aspected at the previous lunation, it will be found that Mercury was in conjunction with one of the planets at the lunation and the lunation made an aspect to Mercury. Therefore, it is seen that Mercury often acts as a "tie-up" planet. Mercury never gets more than 28 degrees away from the Sun as seen from Earth. It has a cycle of approximately eighty-eight days during which time it circles the twelve signs of the zodiac.

Midheaven: This is the name of the cusp of the tenth house in any astrological chart. It is sometimes called the meridian and its abbreviation is MC. This abbreviation is from the two Latin words *Medium Coeli*, which translated literally mean the "middle of the heavens." The Midheaven represents the noon position in clock time. On the Chart of the New York Stock Exchange, this important angle or cusp has always pointed out, by means of planetary transits, every important change in the trend of the stock market. Study well this house and the planets which are in it as well as the aspects to Mars and Neptune, the two planetary rulers of the Midheaven in the New York Stock Exchange Chart at every lunation. It will reveal much concerning the trend of the stock market during the coming twenty-eight days.

Mutable Square: The twelve signs of the zodiac are divided into four elements (fire, water, earth, and air), of three qualities (leading, fixed, and mutable), each. The grouping is as follows:

Fire Signs	*Water Signs*
(Spirit)	(Emotion)
Aries (♈) Leading	Cancer (♋) Leading
Leo (♌) Fixed	Scorpio (♏) Fixed
Sagittarius (♐) Mutable	Pisces (♓) Mutable
Air Signs	*Earth Signs*
(Mind)	(Body)
Libra (♎) Leading	Capricorn (♑) Leading
Aquarius (♒) Fixed	Taurus (♉) Fixed
Gemini (♊) Mutable	Virgo (♍) Mutable

Glossary

The four leading signs form a square (Aries, Cancer, Libra and Capricorn) which have to do with the conscious mind of man.

The four fixed signs form a square (Leo, Scorpio, Aquarius and Taurus) which are related to the sub-conscious mind of man.

The four mutable signs form a square which have to do with the super-conscious mind of man. They are Sagittarius, Pisces, Gemini, and Virgo.

The fire Signs are related to Spirit.

The water signs are related to Emotion.

The air signs are related to Mind.

The earth signs are related to the Physical World. They are practical and materialistic. Planets heavily placed in earth signs turns men's minds toward the material world and its development.

When the mutable square (or the leading or fixed square) is referred to, it signifies the placing of the signs involved on a cross or square. For example the mutable square looks like (a); the leading square like (b); and the fixed square like (c).

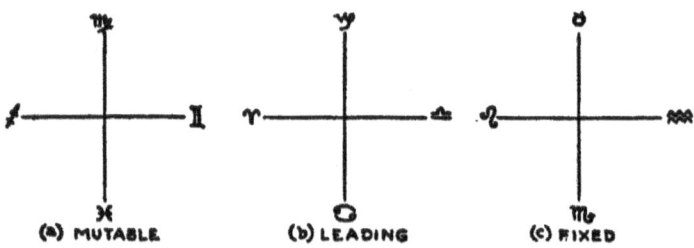

The study of the twelve signs of the zodiac according to this table will reveal more than the study of hundreds of books on the subject. It is especially valuable in giving a quick judgment on the basic makeup of any individual whose birth date you know, and upon whom you wish further information.

New Moon: This is a synonymous term for the lunation or conjunction of the Sun and Moon which occurs every twenty-eight days in one of the twelve signs of the zodiac.

Neptune: This planet moves so slowly that it takes approximately one hundred and sixty-five years to pass through the twelve signs of the zodiac. It passes through a sign about every fourteen years. This means Neptune only moves about 2 degrees a year and 84 seconds a day! Its influence is therefore felt in any degree of the zodiac over a long period of time. In this work Neptune has particular significance because it is the planetary ruler of the sign Pisces, which is ruler of the tenth house or cusp of the Chart of the New York Stock Exchange along with the intercepted sign of Aries. Unfavorable Aspects (conjunction, square, opposition, sesquiquadrate, semi-square) to Neptune at any lunation have usually pointed out a slump or selling wave in stocks during the coming twenty-eight days if there was no favorable aspect between Saturn and Uranus present at the same time to keep the major trend of stocks upward. Watch all aspects to Neptune both at the lunation and from the major planets; they will reveal much about the action of the stock market that is unaccountable in any other way.

North Node: In old books the North Node is sometimes referred to as the "Dragon's Head" and its opposite point called the "Dragon's Tail." The North Node is in reality the point where the orbit of the Moon cuts the ecliptic, as the Moon moves from south into north latitude. The South Node is the point in the zodiac where the Moon crosses from north latitude into south latitude. The North Node is said to have an expansive influence similar to Jupiter and the South Node a restrictive influence similar to the planet Saturn. The Moon's North Node has a cycle of nineteen years; that is, it takes nineteen years for the North Node to pass through the twelve signs of the zodiac. It always moves *backward* through the zodiac. This cycle is highly important and it is taken as the basis for forecasting the rise and fall of business conditions as well as stock market prices. The Business Cycle Chart, as originated by the writer, is based completely on the cycle of the Moon's North Node. Study well the planetary aspects to the North Node as well as the secondary factors present. The trend and conditions of all types of business can be learned in this way.

Opposition: This is an unfavorable aspect or angle between two or more planets placed 180 degrees apart. This means that the planets are placed in opposite signs of the zodiac. The orb of influence for an opposition aspect is 9 degrees. The symbol for the opposition aspect is ☍.

Orb: Sometimes referred to as the "orb of influence" of a planet or aspect, it relates to the distance in degrees in which a planet's influence or aspect can be felt. When the phrase "within orb" is used it means that the planet or aspect has come within the prescribed distance in which its influence can be felt.

Orbit: The path of a planet around the Sun is called its orbit.

Planets: In this work we call the Sun, Moon, Mercury, Venus, Mars, Saturn, Jupiter, Uranus, Neptune, and Pluto the ten planets with which we work.

Pluto: This planet, which was discovered in March 1930, is the latest addition to the list of known planets today. Very little is known of its influence at the present time. It is generally conceded to rule the sign of Scorpio. In this work it has been found to be prominently placed and aspected during booms and depressions; therefore, it is evident that it has significance and influence in the business and financial world with which this work is concerned. During the next ten-year period (1940-1950) Pluto will be in the first 15 degrees of the sign of Leo.

Retrograde: All planets except the Sun and Moon appear to move backward through the zodiac at certain times. When you find a planet marked retrograde (Rx) in the ephemeris, it simply means that from the viewpoint of Earth the planet is apparently moving backward through the signs, instead of forward, or in direct motion.

Ruler: It has been found through research and experience that certain planets have an affinity for certain signs in the zodiac. The

planet which is strongest in a sign is said to be its ruler. The twelve signs with their planetary rulers are given in Chapter III.

Saturn: Saturn is one of the most beautiful planets in the heavens, but its effect on human affairs appears to be restriction and discipline. Saturn has a cycle of thirty years; therefore, it stays in a sign approximately two and a half years. In studying the trend of the stock market, Saturn is particularly significant if it is in aspect with the governmental planet Uranus. Saturn stands for restriction and delay; depression; and poor business. Its symbol is ♄.

Secondary Factor: This term refers to the major planetary aspects which act in connection with the Business Curve (as portrayed by the nineteen-year cycle of the North Node). They have influence, according to their strength, to distort the normal position of the Business Curve from 5 to 20 percent. They can either inflate the Curve or deflate it from the position it would otherwise hold. The most important secondary factors used in this work are the aspects between Saturn and Uranus, and the transit of the major planets through the sign of Gemini, which has strong affinity for the United States.

Semi-sextile: This is a minor favorable aspect of 30 degrees. Its symbol is ⚺. In this work its orb of influence is 3 degrees.

Sesquiquadrate: This aspect or angle between planets placed four and a half signs apart is unfavorable in influence, although it is considered of minor strength. It is an aspect of 135 degrees which has an orb of influence of 3 degrees. Its symbol is ⚼.

Sextile: This aspect or angle between planets placed two signs apart is favorable in influence and has major strength. It is an aspect of 60 degrees which has an orb of influence of 5 degrees. The symbol for the sextile aspect is ✶.

Square: This aspect or angle between planets placed three signs apart is unfavorable in influence and has major strength. It is an aspect of 90 degrees which has an orb of influence of 5 degrees. The symbol for the square aspect is □.

Glossary

Transit: This is the passage or movement of a planet over an important point in a chart.

Transition Period: The Transition Period refers to the Business Cycle Chart given in Chapter I. When the North Node, moving backward through the zodiac, reaches the sign of Scorpio, the Business Curve is said to have reached a Transition Period as the North Node goes through the signs of Scorpio and Libra. This transit marks the gradual upswing of the Business Curve as it slowly moves from Normal to Above Normal business volume and activity. As the North Node reaches the sign of Taurus on this same Business Cycle chart, business activity again experiences a Transition Period, as the Curve of business volume swings slowly downward from Normal to Below Normal activity and prices.

Trine: This aspect or angle between planets placed four signs apart is favorable in influence and has major strength. It is an aspect of 120 degrees which has an orb of influence of 3 degrees in this work The symbol for the trine aspect, which is considered the most favorable of all aspects is △.

Uranus: This planet, which was discovered in March 1871, has been found to have particular significance in relation to finance and business. It also has strong affinity for governmental matters and those placed at the head of the government. When in aspect with the planet Saturn, it has a marked effect on stock market prices, depending upon the nature of the aspect existing between the two planets. It has a cycle of eighty-four years and therefore takes approximately seven years to pass through one sign of the zodiac. It is sudden, changeful, independent, and revolutionary in nature. The symbol for Uranus is ♅. It rules the sign of Aquarius.

Venus: Venus has only a minor planetary influence in this work in relation to business, finance, and the stock market. Like Mercury, it is often a tie-up planet at a lunation bringing into play major planetary aspects that were otherwise dormant. Watch the transit of Venus over the Midheaven and the Ascendant of the New York Stock Exchange Chart. Bond prices are often at their highest under the transit of this planet over the Midheaven of the chart. Venus has a cycle of two hundred and twenty-four days; that is, it passes through the twelve signs of the zodiac during this time. It is benefic in nature and has much the same influence as the planet Jupiter, although to a lesser degree. Venus rules all industry which has to do with the artistic, feminine, and beautiful. The symbol for Venus is ♀. It has rulership over the signs of Taurus and Libra.

Zodiac: This is a narrow belt around the heavens, divided into twelve signs of 30 degrees longitude each, through which the planets transit.

Glossary

Sign Rulership of Countries

Business and finance in this country is strongly influenced at times by world economic conditions. It is, therefore, advantageous to know the sign rulership of the various nations of the world. The transit of the major planets through these signs mark out history for these countries as though it were handwriting on the wall.

* * * * *

Countries under the influence of Aries: England, Denmark, Judea, Germany, Peru

Countries under the influence of Taurus: Italy, Ireland, Persia, Chili

Countries under the influence of Gemini: United States, Wales, Egypt

Countries under the influence of Cancer: China, Africa, Holland

Countries under the influence of Leo: France, Australia

Countries under the influence of Virgo: Switzerland, Turkey, Uruguay

Countries under the influence of Libra: Japan, Upper Egypt, Argentine Republic, Austria

Countries under the influence of Scorpio: Morocco, Brazil

Countries under the influence of Sagittarius: Spain, Arabia

Countries under the influence of Capricorn: India, New Zealand, Mexico

Countries under the influence of Aquarius: Russia, Sweden, Prussia

Countries under the influence of Pisces: Portugal, some parts of Mexico

Sign Rulership of Countries

As the various planets transit the twelve signs of the zodiac, certain marked effects are noticeable in the country ruled by the sign which experiences the transit. Briefly, these are as follows:

Jupiter: The passage of Jupiter through a country's ruling sign marks a period of prosperity for that country with an expansion of industry, rising prices and general well-being, unless there is a strongly unfavorable aspect to Jupiter present at the same time.

Saturn: The passage of Saturn through a country's ruling sign brings depression, war, crop failures, depressed stock market prices and bond values, disaster, loss, and trouble.

Uranus: The passage of Uranus through a country's ruling sign brings about the most revolutionary and epoch-making changes known. The old form of government is usually discarded for a more liberal form of government. Panics often occur with complete collapse of the country's financial structure following. Strikes and labor difficulties and much discontent among the people are common during this transit. If the country does not become involved in war with a foreign country, it usually suffers civil war or internal upheavals.

Neptune: This planet brings about internal disintegration, chaos, upheavals of a political and religious nature, panics, anarchy, plots against the governmental heads, inflation followed by a complete financial collapse of the country's financial interests.

Mars, Venus and Mercury move so fast that their effects on a country is felt mainly through conjunction with one of the above major planets.

Pluto: So little is known at the present time about the planet Pluto that its effects cannot be listed with certainty. However, it can be said that it has a marked influence on business and financial conditions in this country and when it is favorably aspected by one of the major planets it can lift the Business Curve sharply; when in unfavorable aspect, depress the Business Curve in the same extreme manner.

www.ingramcontent.com/pod-product-compliance
Lightning Source LLC
Chambersburg PA
CBHW030111010526
44116CB00005B/201